You take the blue pill—the story ends, you wake up in your bed and believe whatever you want to believe.

You take the red pill—you stay in Wonderland, and I show you how deep the rabbit hole goes.

Remember: all I'm offering is the truth.

(The Matrix)

TOR & DARKNET
4 DONKEYS

A PRACTICAL BEGINNER'S GUIDE TO THE SECRETS OF DEEPWEB, INTERNET & WEB

Samuel K.

CONTENTS

Acknowledges

I would like to thank all the readers who have chosen this book that I wrote hoping to help you to improve y to improve the knowledge of the hidden world of the internet.

If you enjoy this book, I kindly ask you to write a short review on Amazon so that I can improve my work even more with the next publications.

Thanks!

Sam

CHAPTER ONE
INTRODUCTION TO DARKNET

The Secret World of the Darknet isn't entered via any gate, but throughout the TOR: TOR stands for"The Onion Router". The term"onion" identifies the layers that have to be penetrated from the information: Unlike ordinary browsing, the pc doesn't connect directly to the server where the site is situated. First, a complete chain of servers takes part in the link to produce the best possible anonymity.

The path Of a petition within the TOR system in simplified form.

The layers of this"Onion"

The starting point

Your Journey into a Deep Web page begins in your own pc

The first Coating: Entry-Point

The entrance Stage (Server 1) to the TOR system receives

the IP address from the PC. The TOR customer then connects your personal computer to some other server (server 2), the node. All information is encrypted on the way for this node.

The Second coating: TOR nodes:

The node (Server 2) just knows the entrance node - although not your pc or your own IP address. The information sent through this node is encrypted and therefore can't be read by the node. Besides the entrance stage, the TOR node only knows the exit node (Server 3), i.e. the host that connects you to the page.

The third Twist: Exit Node

The exit node (server 3) determines the true connection to the internet server where the requested goal page is situated. In the exit node, you are able to get the valid services that finish in .onion. Away from the TOR community, services together with the .onion expansion aren't available.

The Goal: Internet server

This is Wherever your trip ends - you have reached your

destination. This is the point where the Deep webpage that you would like to get is saved. This internet server only knows the IP address of the exit node. The web server doesn't have to know the additional servers along with your PC.

The information Packets between the notebook and the entrance point are all encrypted. The entry point gets the encrypted package, repacks it, adds the speech of this TOR node and its sender IP address. It then sends the package into the TOR node, which essentially does the exact same thing: it doesn't open the package but flags its IP address as the sender also sends the entire thing on into the speech of the exit node. This manner, the IP address of the source device stays secure because the site just knows the address of the exit node and every one of those individual cases only knows its closest neighbor. In this manner, the user remains anonymous.

Of Course, you could even get"ordinary" clear webpages through the TOR browser. With normal web pages, TOR acts like an ordinary browser. With profound web pages it seems somewhat different: Given the sophistication and higher number of links required, it is hardly surprising that obtaining a profound web page requires considerably longer than accessing a standard site.

HTTP vs. HTTPS

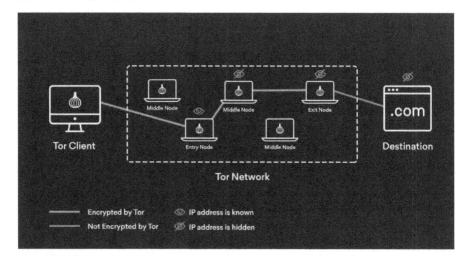

HTTP

HyperText Transfer Protocol (HTTP)

Ahead of the real URL, the abbreviation HTTP looks in the very top from the browser's address bar.

The link isn't encrypted. Hackers have a simple time intercepting, manipulating and reading the information.

The TOR browser sets the end to HTTP connections. After entering an HTTP address, the browser asks a securely encrypted HTPPS edition of the webpage.

HTTPS

HyperText Transfer Protocol Secure (HTTPS)

The URL is preceded by HTTPS and also usually a little padlock icon to signify the safety of their relationship.

To boost the safety of HTTP connections, the SSL certificate was added. The computers communicating with each other agree on a frequent secret that protects the relationship.

The manufacturers of TOR consider HTTP to be so insecure they mechanically join a certificate to every HTTP link, thus transforming it in an HTTPS connection.

Is your consumer completely protected with TOR?

The TOR Browser and similar programs make the avenues taken from the information anonymous. On the other hand, the information sent via it isn't necessarily protected. By way of instance, log-in info, credit card data or addresses could be extracted when inputting data in a web form even when TOR is utilized. Additionally, the anonymity of TOR communicating may also be eliminated if a person gains access into this TOR browser, which could also be manipulated just like any additional applications. Exactly the same applies, obviously, to servers whereby TOR sends users or about what Deep Web pages are saved.

The TOR browser paths a petition Through several nodes. From the perspective of the destination node, this petition comes in the Czech Republic.

Two options to TOR:

Though TOR is the best-known way for Anonymizing traffic, it's not the only protocol that may ensure the anonymity of consumers from the deep website.

Hornet (Highspeed Onion Routing Network) The anonymization system developed by investigators in the University College London and ETH Zurich is comparable to TOR in performance but works quicker.

I2P (Invisible Internet Project) I2P, on the other hand, functions in principle such as a virtual private network - and is therefore distinct from TOR and Hornet.

What's the gap between Darknet and Deep Web?

In most of the favorite German-language networking, the phrases Darknet And Deep Internet are used synonymously. In fact, Darknet and Deep Internet are by no means equivalent since the Darknet is just a little portion of the Internet.

Figuratively we could envision the Web such as this: The normal Web, which we could hunt with Google and Co., is the tip of this iceberg. The component underwater, which we may only see with specific means, is that the Deep Web., along with also the Darknet is the bottom of the iceberg floating in the ocean.

To see the Areas of the iceberg under the surface, special "diving equipment" is needed - the TOR-Browser. To get in the Internet to Darknet, more is demanded. While the observable net - i.e. the recognizable, observable and search engine driven Web - is reachable with a typical browser, the profound web operates hidden under the top layer of the network. To access the webpages of the Deep Internet you require collateral, the TOR system, which implies anonymity while browsing. The sole access secret to the Web is a particular software and the proper browser settings.

Who is utilizing the darknet?

Anonymity is especially interesting for two classes: On the 1 hand, there Are individuals who want the security of the Deep Web because of their own communications. They discuss sensitive information and data and need to fear for their lives or those of the informants if they don't exchange data under the security of the Internet. This group involves the oppressed or dissidents, opposition members out of nations led by dictators or journalists and whistleblowers. Throughout the Deep Web, they're also able to get content that isn't readily available to them to the observable web as a result of governmental restrictions, that's censored, or which could set the informant's life in danger.

Anonymization helps journalists shield their resources. By Way of Example, Arab Spring activists have managed to get social networking stations throughout the TOR system and disseminate information regarding the revolution. Whistleblowers like Edward Snowden additionally use the Internet to deliver sensitive data to the general public. This original class protects itself from unwanted effects and persecution by visiting the Web.

And the next group also utilizes the anonymity of the Deep Web to escape Negative effects - and - escape prosecution. This group consists of individuals whose actions on the observable Web would very quickly result in complaints, penalties and imprisonment. Darknet includes forums, internet stores and trading platforms for both goods and services which are either prohibited or subject to strict regulations.

Which are Hidden Services?

Hidden solutions are computers Which Make their functionality available within The TOR community and whose speech ends in .onion. Their purpose may be a very simple web server or even an intricate service composed of numerous modules. Hidden solutions incorporate all internet content that can't be found through search engines. Additionally, this includes Clear Internet pages which aren't found for Google and Co.. Anybody who knows the URL, i.e. that the www speech, of these pages may call them up with no issues - Google, on the other hand, can't discover them. Strictly speaking, even pages that are relatively simple to monitor are part of the Deep Web.

Specifically, pages with content that is illegal, such as transshipment points for Firearms and drugs or sites for child porn, are one of the so-called "hidden providers" of the Internet: they're accessible via a standard browser are they insured by normal search engines. However, not all of the concealed providers are prohibited: some email providers utilize hidden services to supply highly protected traffic. Such as the Internet, concealed providers have 2 sides.

And what would be the offenders performing in the Darknet?

Unregistered weapons, drugs, stolen and forged records or credit cards: In The Darknet there's everything which shouldn't be accessible under the present law. Increasingly, IT specialists with criminal aspirations will also be offering their services from the Darknet. From overload attacks (DDoS attacks) made to paralyze sites and Web services to virus construction kits and junk campaigns - Darknet is shopping heaven for cybercriminals. Payment is generally created in one of those many electronic crypto monies, which can also be created for anonymity.

A Number of the underground forums Utilize a recommended method to approve new Retailers. New consumers are just admitted as retailers should they've been categorized as trusted from other, currently active retailers. Sometimes, clients also must be accepted by the owner, pay a"membership fee" or a deposit until they could view anything on the website and make purchases.

Considering that the consumers in Darknet go virtually without a trace, researchers can simply Monitor the perpetrators behind the offender offers, online stores or forums at the Darknet after extended research. Because of this, investigating police have established particular units whose job it is to permeate the prohibited regions of the Darknet. Timeless surveillance work can also be among the tools utilized to capture the perpetrators: Medication prices, by way of instance, are usually carried out through packaging channels, as in the instance of"Moritz". The very fact that access cards to the Packstation which were stolen and sold from the Darknet are often used for these trades makes the offender net of their Darknet evident.

What's possible from the Darknet?

From the Darknet, what's potential That's possible on the publicly Available Internet. Moreover, the anonymity of the Darknet opens nearly infinite possibilities to provide services that are prohibited, killings, weapons and drugs or to discuss or obtain pornographic articles of any sort and videos of both murders and misuse.

What you Can Purchase on the Darknet:

Deadly poison

In the United States, this situation made the headlines: a young guy improved his pocket Money with the creation and purchase of ricin. Ricin is a protein derived from a spurge plant that kills human cells and may be deadly even in tiny quantities.

Credit card amounts

These might have fallen into the hands of criminals via phishing sites, Keyloggers or traditional card theft. With this information, the perpetrators can store in the cardholder's expense. Normally the amounts are offered in bulk. This raises the likelihood that at least a few of these cards aren't yet blocked.

Weapons and ordnance

The Darknet contains nearly everything that offenders are searching for. One of the Other items, relevant deep internet sites provides explosives. Besides C4 plastic explosives, rocket launchers and many other weapons may also be bought on the Darknet.

Counterfeit identity cards

A Darknet website called"Fake Records Service" claims in order To provide stolen passports and files out of virtually every nation. A passport of a taxpayer from the USA can be obtained therefor under a million bucks.

Marihuana

The question"How to Purchase weed on the Internet" contributes to nearly one Million hits in the normal Google search. Where there's such a playful demand, there's also a nearly inexhaustible source: From the Darknet, dealers offer you various kinds and forms of this medication. Exactly the same applies to other medications. Everything inflow on the road has since found its way to the Deep Web.

Forged university records

The Darknet is famous for its broad assortment of forgeries of all types. No Wonder, then, that files can be gotten there in a relatively straightforward method. Nonetheless, this isn't a specialty of the Internet: Criminals have been supplying all sorts of forgeries online, which is discovered through Google.

Deal killers

From the Darknet that there are many offers to kill an individual for cash. But, it's uncertain how a lot of these offers are fake or real.

Viruses and malware

The Darknet also boosts cybercrime: With so-called crimeware kits, the Perpetrators can arrange malware and viruses based on their own wishes, with no in-depth understanding, with only a couple of clicks.

Uranium

In a world where nearly everything could be bought, It's hardly surprising That uranium ore, which may be processed to weapons, may also be acquired on the Darknet. The Washington Post has researched such supplies. The editors have discovered that the uranium ores which can be found in tiny amounts on the Darknet can also be available from Amazon.

Which search engines are there for your own Darknet?

These search engines search the shadowy net for concealed services and so for Sites end in".onion".

Grams

The most famous search engine for Darknet is named Grams. Its emblem is based on the Google logo concerning color, and the arrangement of the result pages is as easy to use as Google. While Grams looks like Google optically, the search results are somewhat less standard: Grams is chiefly utilized for research queries regarding drug trafficking, but also for hunting for firearms, stolen credit cards, hacker providers and contract killings.

ahmia.fi

Ahmia has made it it's business to filter out all outcomes on child pornography From the search results and not to display them. Thus Ahmia.fi is among those very few Deep search engines to draw at least a thin moral line. Together with the proper technical prerequisites, Ahmia may also be incorporated as an add-on in most popular browsers.

Torch

The search results are presented in precisely the exact same manner as Google. In accordance with Torch, it's more than ten million active users, which can be due to it being promoted on the file-sharing website The Pirate Bay. The operators of these professional services end with. Onion should actively enroll their pages in a directory that can then be searched by search engines like Torch, Grams and ahmia.fi.

Can I make myself liable to prosecution when I browse in the Darknet?

Search engines like Grams, ahimia.fi and Torch assist users to look for the As unmanageable Darknet at a targeted manner - like Google and Co.. Facilitate the search for internet content.

Both surfing and searching the dark net can become harmful: Even without purchasing illegal products and services, Darknet users may make themselves liable to prosecution when the thumbnails, i.e. the small preview pictures of their lookup outcome, wind up at the browser cache and are therefore saved onto the computer even if just temporarily. If researchers find these thumbnails of illegal material like child porn, this is sufficient for prosecution. So as to avert this, users typically use a virtual private network (VPN) that averts the storage of information. The genuine surfing at the Darknet is hence prohibited per se - it is dependent on what you are doing there.

CHAPTER TWO
ACCESSING THE DARKNET / DARK WEB

The Net has turned into a baseline necessity of running the business. Whether assessing email, catching up on business news or obtaining customer information, the majority of us utilize the net through the day, daily, in many different capacities. However, do we know how it functions, even at a fundamental level? To be able to better clarify the darknet and the dark web, let us begin with a summary of the world wide web.

The expression Net is brief for internetwork, a platform made by linking a range of computer programs together. A web allows for communication between devices which are part of the internetwork.

The Net, which until lately was denoted by a capital "I", is the most famous illustration of an internetwork. This is the net that we find crucial to our everyday lives, and it joins countless devices throughout the world through a network of programs using standardized protocol or procedures.

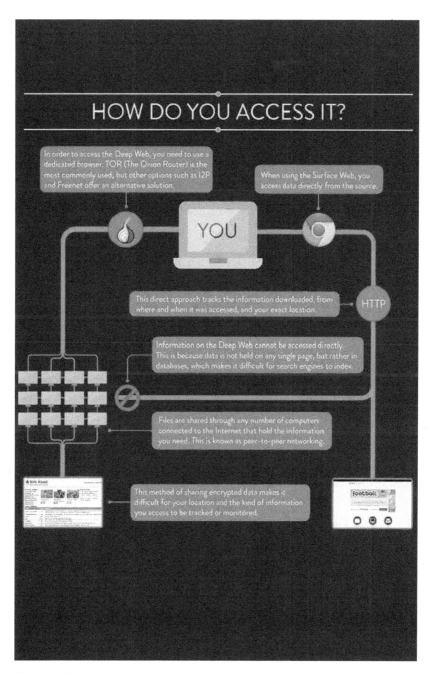

The Online

Browsing Sites on the internet isn't the sole manner in which information is shared through the net. Email, instant messaging, and FTP are different methods to share information such as messages, emails, and documents.

To Clarify, the internet isn't synonymous with the web and ought not to be confused with that. The internet is merely a method of accessing webpages across the medium of the net.

The Surface Internet

The Sites we navigate daily constitute only a small number of the world wide web.

All these Websites, collectively called the surface net, are visible and available to ordinary search engines like Google and Yahoo. While estimates vary, many experts concur that the surface net comprises roughly 4 percent of online content. For more information on the way search engines crawl and index content, visit Google's superb overview.

Under the Surface

Past The surface net, 96 percent of internet content is located from the deep net and also the darknet.

THE DEEP WEB

The deep net is composed of particles that can't be found or straight obtained via surface search engines like Google and Yahoo. Examples of heavy sites include sites which demand credentials (registration and login), unlinked websites which call for an immediate connection to accessibility, websites which are intentionally designed to maintain out search crawlers, and databases - that the vast majority of articles from the deep net.

Deep web Databases commonly possess their own search functionality that lets users access the information contained inside them. Government databases (we will get to an instance in a moment), individual records, and library catalogs are only a couple of instances of databases that are deep. When these databases don't need to demand login credentials, a number of them do.

Let us Have a peek at the Denver Property Taxation and Assessment System site. People can use this website to seek property assessment and taxation information by inputting a Denver-based address to the computer system. But if you enter the exact same Denver-based speech into Google or Yahoo (as well as include provisions like'property evaluation' or'tax information'), then you won't discover the outcomes from the Denver Property Taxation and Assessment System site. This database and its own search performance are just one instance of a profound web database that's concealed from surface search engines.

THE DARKNET + THE DARK WEB

Past The deep net is the darknet. The darknet is a system, built-in addition to the web, that's purposefully concealed, meaning it's been designed particularly for anonymity. Contrary to the deep net, the darknet is only available with specific tools and applications - plugins and other protocol outside direct connections or credentials. You can't get into the darknet simply by typing a darknet address in your internet browser.

Most importantly, we Mention the net we refer to and use every day is the most famous instance of a web. Likewise below are some examples of darknets (every links to more info):

· Tor, or The Onion Router, is an overlay network constituted of volunteer-operated servers which makes it possible for people to divide where they're in the Earth, from where they're surfing online. Users link through a string of virtual tunnels instead of creating an immediate link.

· I2P, or even the Invisible Internet Project, is an anonymous overlay network - a system in a community - designed to protect communicating from monitoring and surveillance.

· Freenet is a free program that enables users to anonymously share documents, navigate and release"free sites" (sites reachable only through Freenet) and chat online forums. Communications by Freenet nodes are encrypted and are routed through other nodes to ensure it is extremely hard to ascertain who is requesting the information and what its content is.

· ZeroNet is a good instance of a decentralized community that can also work as a darknet.

We'll use Tor, possibly the very famous and most-used, to better Describe the darknet and shadowy net. Tor, brief for The

Onion Router (the job's unique name), paths traffic to shadowy sites through layers of encryption to permit anonymity. The dark web expression identifies sites on a darknet. In Tor's instance, these darknet addresses all finish in .onion.

Onion routing is employed by tunneled encryption. Tor constructs a virtual Link between the consumer and each host in the path of three Tor relays. Every relay decrypts a layer of encryption to show only another relay so as to pass the residual encrypted information. The closing Tor relay decrypts the innermost layer of encryption and transmits the initial data to its destination without showing, or even understanding, the origin address.

Other darknets Mentioned Previously employ similar Procedures of Information Transmission, with the end goal of maintaining customers, users, and data concealed.

Who Makes the Darknet and Why?

Most of everything you have probably read or heard about the darknet and dim net Sites involves malicious or illegal activity. Obviously, where there are potentially valid applications for anonymity, in addition, there are criminals seeking to utilize the anonymity of the darknet for their benefit, with the most significant volume of darknet websites revolving around drugs, darknet niches (darknet websites for the purchasing and selling of products and services), and fraud. Cases of criminal usage of these darknets are observed below.

CRIMINAL

· Medication or other prohibited chemical traders: A wide variety of darknet markets (black markets) permit for the anonymous purchasing and sale of drugs and other prohibited or controlled substances such as pharmaceuticals.

· Counterfeiters: Counterfeiters provide document forging and money imitation services through the darknet.

· Vendors of stolen data: Credit card numbers and other personally identifiable information (PII) could be bought on the darknet for fraud and theft actions.

· Weapons traders: A wide variety of darknet markets (black markets) permit for the anonymous, illegal selling and buying of weapons.

· Hackers: Black hat hackers, or even people seeking to skip and exploit safety measures for individual gain or just out of needing a company or actions, brag about their exploits, communicate and collaborate with other hackers, and discuss safety loopholes (use a bug or vulnerability to gain access to applications, hardware, information, etc.) about the darknet.

· Gamblers: Certain websites on the darknet block U.S.-based online providers. Gamblers may take into the darknet to skirt local gaming laws.

· Terrorists: As people living or functioning in nations being directed by oppressive regimes will frequently take into the darknet, terrorists also do. Internet accessibility, recruitment, sharing of data, and organizing could be carried out anonymously on the darknet.

· Murderers/Assassins: While there's disagreement as to whether these solutions are valid, law enforcement, or just fictitious websites, you will find dark sites where murder-for-hire providers are recorded.

· Vendors of prohibited explicit stuff: We will not go into further detail.

CHAPTER THREE
STEP BY STEP GUIDE TO SAFELY ACCESSING THE DARK NET AND DEEP WEB

Google only indexes a tiny fraction of the world wide web. By some estimates, the Web includes 500 times more articles than that which Google yields in search results. The hyperlinks which Google and other search engines come back should you type in a question is called the"surface net," while all the other, non-searchable content is known as the"deep web" or"invisible web".

Most of this information is concealed simply because the Huge majority of users will do not find it applicable. A lot of it's tucked away in databases that Google is not interested in or barred from crawling. A good deal of it's old and obsolete. The contents of iPhone programs, the documents on your Dropbox accounts, academic journals, court documents, and personal social networking profiles are examples of information that are not automatically indexed by Google but still exist online.

Caution: Your ISP can discover You're using Tor

A lot of the Report revolves around the usage of anonymity networks such as Tor, Which are utilized to get the dark web.

Internet providers can discover when Tor is used because Tor node IPs are people. If you would like to use Tor independently, you can utilize either a VPN or Tor Bridges (Tor nodes which aren't publicly flashed). US Tor users in particular might want to utilize a VPN, which is quicker and much more dependable.

Recent changes in US laws mean net providers are free to market And share information on their clients, including their surfing habits. When using a VPN, your ISP won't have the ability to realize that you're connected to some Tor entrance node, just an encrypted tunnel to your VPN server.

NordVPN is your #1 option for Tor and continues to be Designed with Tor consumers in your mind.

Deep net vs dark web

The deep web is frequently confused with all the dark web, also known as darknet, Black net, and black web. To put it differently, the deep internet is all the info stored on the internet that is not indexed by search engines. You do not require any special tools or a dim web browser to get into the deep web; you simply have to know where to search. Specialized search engines, directories, and wikis will help users find the information they're searching for.

A number of the very best general deep internet search engines have closed down or been Obtained, such as Alltheweb and CompletePlanet. However, some are hanging about to get you started:

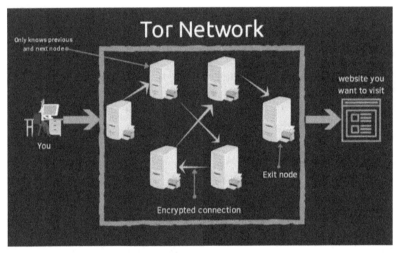

DeeperWeb -- deep search engine which leverages Google Search

The WWW Virtual Library -- The first index of the internet, but more of a directory than a search engine.

Surf wax -- Indexes RSS feeds. Not sure that this is still functioning...

IceRocket -- Searches the blogosphere and Twitter

These are all fine, but technical search engines tend to be better than General ones for locating information on the deep net. If you're trying to find a court case, as an instance, utilize your state or nation's public records search. If you require academic journals, take a look at our post on utilizing deep internet search engines for academic and technical research. The more specific you are, the better, or you'll just end up with exactly the identical search results you would find on Google. Should you want a particular file type, such an Excel document or a PDF, find out how to define searches for that kind of document (e.g. kind"filetype: PDF" on your DeeperWeb query).

The dark web is a little portion of the profound web that's kept hidden on goal. Sites and information on the darknet do typically take a particular tool to get. The kind of website most frequently connected with the darknet are marketplaces where illegal goods like narcotics, guns, and stolen credit card numbers have been purchased and sold. The darkest corners are utilized to engage hitmen, participate in human trafficking, and exchange child pornography. More than this, however, the darknet includes data and content which could be obtained with anonymity. It may be a website, discussion, chat area, or personal gaming server.

The attractiveness of the dark web is anonymity. Nobody

knows who anybody else is in The actual world, as long as they accept the required precautions. Consumers are free from the prying eyes of both corporations and governments.

The darknet and Tor are often used by journalists and whistleblowers to Exchange sensitive information, such as Edward Snowden himself. The Ashley Madison info ditch, for example, was submitted to a website only available to Tor users.

The best way to get the Dark Internet safely

The darknet isn't a single, centralized location. Precisely like the outside net, It's scattered among servers across the world. This guide will teach you how best to get the darknet through Tor, brief for The Onion Router. Dark internet website URLs are usually appended with".onion" instead of ".com" or even ".org", signaling they're only available to Tor users.

Tor Is a system of volunteer relays whereby the consumer's internet connection is routed. The link is encrypted, and the visitors pop between relays located across the world, which makes the user anonymous.

Just just how can you get on the Tor network? The Simplest way is to download and install the Tor Browser. According to

Firefox, you can browse the net exactly as with any other browser, except each of your traffic is routed via the Tor Network. Be certain that you download the Tor Browser just from the official site, lest you risk downloading spyware, malware, or another virus for your device. Officially, the Tor Browser is only available on Windows, Mac, and Linux, so many experts advise against using third-party browsers which use the Tor Network.

The best way to get the darknet on Android using Tor Browser (UPDATE)

The official Tor Browser is currently available on Android. You can get it out of The Play Store or the Tor downloads webpage. As of writing, Tor Browser for Android is still in alpha, and also requires you to set up Orbot for a prerequisite.

The Tor Browser is the most common dark browser. After Tor Browser is installed, now you can get those .onion dark web sites.

Navigating the dark Web

Now you Can safely navigate darknet sites and concealed wikis, but if you intend To do anything longer than that, you will want to take several steps. If you're planning to create a buy on a dark web market like Silk Road to find those medications your dying mother so desperately wants to endure, for example, you will want to create a bogus identity. Meaning setting up encrypted email using a brand new email address, with a pseudonym, establishing an anonymous bitcoin wallet, disabling Javascript from Tor Browser, exploring vendors, and much more.

Evidently, locating these .onion sites is your initial challenge, as they Will not appear in Google search results. You can not simply Google"Silk Road" and aspire to land on the darkened web site. A couple of dark search engines that do indicator .onion websites comprise Onion.city, Onion.to, and NotEvil. To search several marketplaces for particular goods, especially medications and narcotics, there are Grams.

Reddit is also a valuable source for locating the dark web or profound web Website You're searching for. Try out the /r/deep web, /r/onions, and /r/Tor subreddits. Hidden wiki directories similar to this 1 may also be handy to help narrow your search.

We can not emphasize enough that anonymity and security

are overriding To people on shadowy web sites. Your ISP and the authorities may not have the ability to observe your action when on the Tor Network, however, they do understand you're about the Tor Network, which alone is sufficient to raise eyebrows. In reality, a recent ruling from the US Supreme Court denoted that just using Tor was sufficient probable cause for authorities to try to capture any computer across the globe.

Another essential precaution is to make sure your .onion URLs are right. Onion URLs generally have a series of apparently random letters and figures. And as there's hardly any use of HTTPS on the darkened web, verifying whether a site is valid with an SSL certificate isn't possible. We recommend confirming the URL from three distinct sources before utilizing any website on the dark web. When you're sure you have the proper URL, store it into an encrypted notice --that the Tor browser won't cache it for later. Otherwise, there is a fantastic prospect of falling prey to a Millionaire scam similar to this imitation bitcoin mixer.

Because of This, we highly recommend using another layer of safety via a VPN.

VPN over Tor versus Tor over VPN

A VPN allows a user to encrypt All of the Online traffic travel to and Out of her or his device and route it via a server at a location of the user's picking. A VPN in conjunction with Tor, further increases the safety and anonymity of the consumer.

While somewhat similar, Tor highlights ideology, and also a VPN highlights solitude.

Combining them reduces danger, but there is a significant distinction in how Both of these tools socialize. Let us first talk Tor over VPN.

Should you connect to a VPN and flame up Tor Browser, you are using Tor Over VPN, which is undoubtedly the most frequent method. Your entire device's traffic goes into the VPN server, then it circulates via the Tor Network before finishing up at its final destination. Your ISP just sees the encrypted VPN traffic, and also will not understand you are on Tor. You are able to get .onion sites normally.

Tor over VPN needs you hope your VPN supplier, which may see that you Are using Tor and maintain metadata logs, even though it can not really observe the content of your encoded Tor traffic. A logless VPN, that does not store any visitors logs nor session logs is highly preferable. Traffic logs include the information of your traffic, such as lookup queries and sites you visited, whilst session logs include metadata such as your IP address, even when you logged in to the VPN, and also just how much data was moved. Traffic logs are a larger concern than session logs, but are great.

For built-in Tor over VPN performance, NordVPN functions servers that automatically route you via the Tor network. You do not even have to utilize to Tor Browser, but bear in mind other browsers may still pass identifying data through the system.

Tor over VPN also does not shield users from malicious Tor exit nodes. Since Tor nodes comprise of volunteers, not all of them play with the rules. The last relay prior to your traffic travels to the destination site is referred to as the departure node. The exit node decrypts your own traffic and so can steal your private info or inject malicious code. Furthermore, Tor exit nodes tend to be blocked by sites that don't trust them and Tor over VPN can not do anything about this, either.

Then there is the popular VPN over Tor, which Is advised from the official Tor Project. Only two VPN suppliers we know of, AirVPN and BolehVPN, provide this support, but neither of those scores highly for rates. In cases like this, the purchase price of both tools is changed. Internet traffic passes through the Tor Network, then through the VPN. This usually means the VPN supplier does not see your actual IP address, as well as the VPN, protects you away from these lousy exit nodes.

Tor over VPN needs you to put any hope on your VPN supplier but not your ISP and is greatest if you would like to get .onion sites. VPN over Tor needs you to put trust on your ISP but maybe not your own VPN and is greatest if you would like to prevent poor Tor exit nodes. Some belief VPN over Tor more protected since it preserves anonymity during the whole procedure (assuming you cover your VPN anonymously). Even though the official Tor Project advises against VPN over Tor, the two approaches are superior not to using a VPN in any way.

The significant caveat is a rate. Because of all of the nodes Your traffic moves Through, Tor alone considerably restricts bandwidth. Adding a VPN for it, even only a fast 1 such as IPVanish can make it slower, so please be patient.

I2P

I2P is an Alternate Anonymous community to Tor. Contrary

to Tor, nevertheless, it can't be used to get the public net. It may simply be used to get hidden services particularly to the I2P network. I2P can't be utilized to get .onion websites since it's an entirely different network from Tor. Rather, I2P uses its own brand of concealed websites called"eepsites".

So why can you use I2P rather than Tor? In the end, it is not as popular, Can not be utilized to get normal sites, and is not as simple to use, among other advantages. Both rely upon a peer-to-peer routing arrangement along with layered encryption to create browsing anonymous and private.

I2P has a few benefits, however. It is much faster and reliable than Tor for numerous technical factors. The peer-reviewed routing arrangement is much more advanced and it doesn't rely upon a reliable directory to find route details. I2P uses one-way channels, so that an eavesdropper can simply capture inbound or outbound visitors, not.

Establishing I2P requires more configuration on the consumer's role than Tor. I2P has to be downloaded and installed, and then setup is done via the router. Then individual programs must each be configured to operate with I2P. On an internet browser, then you will want to configure your browser proxy settings to use the appropriate port.

Freenet

Much like I2P, Freenet is a midsize network inside the community which can not Be used to access websites online web. It may simply be used to get the material uploaded into the Freenet, and it is a peer-to-peer dispersed datastore. Contrary to I2P and Tor, you do not require a host to host articles. As soon as you upload something, it remains there indefinitely, even if you quit using Freenet, so long as it's popular.

Freenet enables users to attach in one of 2 manners: darknet and opennet. Darknet mode permits you to define who your friends are around the community and just join and share content together. This enables groups of individuals to make closed, anonymous networks composed only of people they trust and know.

Otherwise, consumers can connect into an opennet manner, which automatically Assigns peers on the community. Unlike darknet style, opennet utilizes a couple of servers that are dedicated along with the decentralized peer-reviewed community.

The configuration is quite straightforward. Simply download, install, and operate. When you start your default browser, Freenet is going to be prepared and running via its interface. Notice that you need to use another browser than the one you usually use to make sure anonymity.

Freenet remains an experiment designed to withstand denial-of-service strikes and censorship.

Google & Bing know everything virtually. Why just"nearly"? Having a market share of about 92 percent Google is the best performer among the various search engines, Bing with roughly 3 percent is obviously beaten to put two, but clearly before other candidates. Both search engines catch all of their information automatically and therefore are for at least 95 percent of the planet's inhabitants the beginning page to the net.

Everything that appears on the very first pages is visible Online and is Clicked by users. Everything else is dismissed. But all results accumulated by Google & Co. aren't complete. How many percentages of the world wide web isn't indexed by search engines isn't known. It's also rather easy to conceal a web site from Google & Co..

What is the Deep Web?

Everything which isn't found by search engines is known as"Deep Web". And Then there's a specially encrypted place on the internet, the so-called darknet. Incidentally, this isn't just for prohibited purposes. Technically that the Darknet is a portion of the Deep Web. It's also occasionally called"Hidden Web", and at times the words Darknet and Deep Internet are used synonymously.

Is your darknet illegal?

No, the darknet isn't illegal. On the opposite: the Darknet is just one of those last bastions of freedom of speech, or so the system can be used globally by journalists, human rights organizations, regime critics and repressed minorities. At precisely the exact same time, but it's unfortunately also a playground for offenders.

The Darknet is a community with no censorship and surveillance -- together with its benefits and pitfalls. By way of instance, some newspapers such as the New York Times have put up their own webpages in Darknet so that informants can transmit confidential data anonymously.

Incidentally, famous IT journalists such as Mike Tigas possess their own Homepage in Darknet -- however, that exists"on the standard" Internet.

What and where is the darknet?

How do I get into the Darknet? Is Darknet banned? -- These are likely the Usual queries in connection with this component of the world wide web. Darknet employs the very same areas of the Web that all other Web providers utilize: Sites, email and document sharing. All this, like the rest of the web, is publicly accessible -- you just need to understand how to get there and the place to hunt.

If You Would like to browse the Darknet, you need anonymous access to this Tor Network. Tor is initially an abbreviation for"The Onion Router" and it's a community for anonymizing relationship information, that was in operation since about 2002 and has been chiefly developed by students at Cambridge University. You'll have the ability to read the word"onion" a few times from the subsequent post.

The Term berry is a reference to the various layers that Need to pass Via the information en route by the consumer to the site: There's almost always a whole chain of servers included in the relation between the user and the host so as to produce the best possible anonymity. Presently, about 2 million people use the Tor system daily.

Concerning the technical heritage of the Tor system, anyone who hunts the "normal" Web, e.g. Google, is attached directly to Google with their particular IP address. From the Tor system, you will find three additional servers (so-called"nodes") involving your IP along with the web site that you need to see, and it's thus not possible to follow where the visitor comes from. The source code where the Darknet relies on open source and may be seen by everybody. If you'd like, you could also actively take part and supply your personal server, which acts as an anonymous node from the dark web or Tor network. Obviously, it's also possible to place your pages to Darknet.

What's a Tor Browser?

The Tor Browser is a unique version of Firefox that automatically selects The Tor system as the online access point. The Tor Browser can also be contained within our Windows compatible Cyber Shield program!

Also, for additional operating systems along with your cell phone, you will find alternatives for Darknet plugins to download, e.g. that the"Tor Browser" for MacOS, the"Onion Browser" to get iPhone & iPad and Orfox, Orbot or"Tor Browser" -- for Android. You most likely have the widest choice for a consumer of a device under Android.

But we urge the version within our applications Cyber Shield, as the Tor Browser in this variant is also doubly secured without the access to a computer that can occur!

Darknet: Please be cautious!

As anywhere in life, you need to bring a healthy Part of skepticism when Employing the Darknet. Where no censorship or surveillance is possible, you'll also discover a lot of shady characters. However, there aren't just trading areas for weapons or drugs! So seeing Darknet department stores might not be the best thought.

You should not provide your personal data everywhere and you should not upload Self-created images & videos everywhere. Downloads from Darknet are possibly dangerous and you should not purchase anything in Darknet. Do your self a favor.

Simply do not believe or trust anybody when browsing Darknet! Recall: Another Users are anonymous also! At times it's even a good idea to conceal your webcam if you proceed from the Darknet. But that may be a bit overly paranoid.

We hope we did not scare you today? However, a little caution can not hurt while Surfing the Darknet!

Guide throughout the Darknet

In Darknet, you will find none of the typical domains together with all the endings. com, . net, . Org or comparable. The expansion used in Darknet is .Onion.

The hottest page in Darkweb is most likely the Onion edition of Facebook. This page permits you to use Facebook anonymously without the fear of monitoring. This support is also the only alternative for individuals from countries such as China, Iran or any African nations where Facebook is censored and blocked.

The address is: https://www.facebookcorewwwi.onion/

Many sites in Darknet do not stay online very long. That is why the Darknet -- such as the rest of the Web -- also has search engines and less or more up-to-date connection lists.

The best Dog at the Darknet search engines was Grams for quite a while. Nearly the Google of Darknet. With Grams it had been possible to seek the Darknet -- and it seemed quite similar. Whereby Grams didn't actively hunt the Darknet alone, however, a site always needed to be enrolled with Grams first. However, Grams has vanished from the scene for many months now.

A recent option is Torch. The present speech of Torch is http://xmh57jrzrnw6insl.onion

Wiki Links (http://wikilink77h7lrbi.onion/), deep Weblinks (http://deepppr5ooheo7n6.onion/), OnionDir, Tor Links or Hidden Wiki (http://zqktlwi4fecvo6ri.onion) are normal link directories, together with their benefits and pitfalls.

And do not Be amazed: The sites and connect portals in Darknet remind one of the sites from the 90s of the past millennium. So the Darknet may make a relaxing setting.

Obviously, there's also an email in the Darknet! 1 supplier is e.g. TorBox, where you can make an anonymous account at no cost. However, you may just send and receive e-mails inside the Darknet. The service may be reached at the following address http://torbox3uiot6wchz.onion/

if you would like to earn cash transfers in Darknet, then you need to look for services such as OnionWallet. OnionWallet & Co. behave like PayPal and resemble an electronic handbag. The URL to the Bitcoins currency box is as follows: http://aewfdl3tyohbcenp.onion/

An   Option   is   e.g   EasyCoin: http://ts4cwattzgsiitv7.onion/

The"dark web" and"darknet " connote A subset of key sites that exist within an encrypted network.

Even Though the World Wide Web dominates almost every aspect of our daily lives at this time, it is important not to forget that it's only existed for a couple decades. Even though this is a comparatively brief length of time compared with the length of human history, it's a large number of technological lifetimes. Therefore, the world wide web is an exceptionally amazing place, a period of countless individual websites that are linked to one another in a complex blend of means.

The Most Well-known Sites, such as Facebook (FB), Google (GOOG) and Amazon (AMZN) are well-known across the world. Apart from those popular websites, there is a far bigger collection of less-traveled areas of the world wide web. And lurking beyond each the fundamental, accessible regions of the net are different pockets of websites. These past groups constitute the so-called"dark web" or"dark web."

'Dark Web' Versus'Deep Web'

The phrases"dark web" and "darknet " are sometimes used interchangeably but with subtle differences in meaning. They naturally connote a subset of sites that exist in a community that's encrypted.

That the system is encrypted signifies that it Isn't searchable with Traditional means, as an internet search engine, and it is not visible through conventional web browsers. Dark baits exist in several types, and the expression itself does not necessarily imply any nefarious undertones. Dark web is any kind of overlay network that requires specific consent or tools to get.

Why would individuals desire to host sites on the dark web? Dark baits are Commonly associated with many different unique purposes. They may be utilized for lots of crimes, such as illegal file sharing, black markets, as well as a way for the trade of prohibited products or services. These are frequently the most highly-publicized applications of dark web.

However, they're also employed to get a host of different explanations. Dark baits are often Called upon as a way of protecting political dissidents out of reprisal, or as an instrument for permitting people to bypass censorship networks. They could ease whistleblowing and information flows, and they can help protect people from surveillance. Therefore, and due to the great number of software of dark web, they're a hotly contested issue.

"Dark internet" is usually confused with the "deep web." The Deep net identifies unindexed websites that are unsearchable; in the majority of situations, this is because these websites are guarded by passwords. "Dark internet" websites are intentionally concealed from the surface internet in additional ways. A huge majority of sites constitute the"deep web," since they're password-protected.

Encryption as well as the Dark Web

Some of the common methods that dark baits are split from the surface internet is through encryption. Most dark sites utilize the Tor encryption instrument to help conceal their identity.

Tor Enables individuals to conceal their place, appearing like they are in a Different nation. Tor-encrypted networks demand that people use Tor so as to see them. Therefore, those users' IP addresses and other identifying info is encrypted. All this combines to imply that many people can see websites on the dark web, provided that they have the right encryption tools. However, it can be unbelievably difficult to ascertain who oversees those websites. Additionally, it suggests that, if anybody engaging in the dark web has their identity revealed, it could be harmful.

Tor uses layers and layers of encryption, securing traffic by Routing it via a dense network of protected relays to anonymize it. Tor isn't illegal applications in and of itself, in precisely the exact same manner that torrenting tools aren't prohibited. (See also: How Can BitTorrent Sites like The Pirate Bay Make

Money?) In the instances, however, the computer software is often utilized to run illegal action (either through the darkened net or, even in the instance of torrenting tools, to obtain pirated material).

To place Tor's dark web links in context, It's useful to Keep in Mind That Tor Quotes only about 4 percent of its visitors is used for dim net services, together with the rest simply accounted for by people accessing routine sites with a higher level of anonymity and security.

Infamous Cases of this Dark Web

When most People Today think of this dark web, a couple of notable examples come to mind. These are websites or networks of websites that are made headlines for just one reason or another. Most are prohibited for a couple of reasons. But, there are additional possible darknets, rather than all of them are always prohibited.

Among the Most Well-known examples of a darkened community was that the Silk Road marketplace. Silk Road has been a site used for the purchasing and selling of many different illegal things, such as recreational firearms and drugs.

Silk Road Was set in 2011 and is often considered the initial dim net sector. Even though it was closed down by authorities in 2013, it's spawned a variety of copycat markets.

Marketplaces like Silk Road were instrumental in the development of Cryptocurrencies, the majority of which rely upon decentralization and improved safety measures. The anonymity and privacy of several cryptocurrencies have made them the option of option when completing trades in dark markets.

Reasons to Use or Avoid the Dark Web

Besides prohibited purchases and sales, there are valid reasons one may Be interested in utilizing the dark web. People within closed societies and confronting intense censorship can use the dark web to communicate with other people beyond society. Even people within open societies might have some interest in utilizing the dark web, especially as concerns regarding government snooping and data collection continue to rise globally.

However, a large part of the action that Occurs on the Dark

Net is prohibited. It is not tough to surmise why this could be the situation: the dark web offers a degree of individuality safety the surface internet doesn't. Criminals seeking to secure their identities so as to prevent detection and capture have been attracted to the facet of the dark web. Because of this, it is unsurprising that several noteworthy hacks and information breaches are linked with the dark web in some manner or another.

In 2015, as an example, a trove of consumer info was stolen out of Ashley Madison, a site purporting to provide spouses a way of cheating on their spouses. The stolen information showed on the dark web, where it was later recovered and shared with the general public. In 2016, then-U.S. Attorney General Loretta Lynch cautioned that gun sales happening over the dark internet were becoming more prevalent, as it enabled buyers and sellers to prevent regulations. Illegal pornography is another relatively common occurrence on the dim web.

Thinking about the nefarious underbelly of this dark web, it is Not Surprising that Most individuals don't have any reason to get it. And given the greater importance of cryptocurrencies from the monetary world, it is likely that dim nets will get more of a characteristic for ordinary internet users later on.

Meanwhile, they might also still supply offenders a way of eluding capture, though accurate anonymity is not guaranteed, even if utilizing encryption of the kind found in those networks.

****

Are you enjoying this book? If so, please let me know your thoughts by leaving a short review on Amazon.

It means a lot to me!

Thanks!

Sam

CHAPTER FOUR
BRIGHT SPOTS ON THE DARKNET

The darknet is not all creepy, prohibited content. There is definitely no Lack of criminal malware or forums marketplaces under the surface net, but there is also a few valid sites and communities.

To be clear, the darknet Remains, well, dangerous and dark. You should not simply download a Tor browser and go digging for hazard intelligence. Not everybody who heads under the surface net, however, is hoping to purchase stolen passwords or lease a botnet for hire. Some Tor consumers are just hoping to read the information, get an ad-free search encounter or play a game of chess.

Bear in mind, the darknet isn't like the deep net. The deep net includes Any services which are not available to the public, such as corporate intranet webpages or internet banking portals. The darknet is described as sites and services which are not found by major search engines or reachable by ordinary browsers. It is estimated that there are somewhere between 10,000 and 100,000 sites on the darknet, based on TechRepublic.

Globally, there are approximately two million users of this Tor browser. A number of these Tor users are up to no good. Others only wish to navigate the surface net anonymously, or sometimes contribute to healthy darknet content.

10 Bright Spots around the Darknet

While there is no shortage of dreadful content Beneath the surface of this Net, in addition, there are some sites that have real value to the general attention. Others are enlightening or just entertaining. Listed below are 10 bright places to keep a lookout for on the darknet.

Note: Prevent trying to get. Onion websites from a surface net browser And proceed with care.

1. The Chess

"The Chess" is a dark site devoted to completely anonymous games of chess, Played real-time against a stranger. When you make an account, then you are able to take part in boundless gaming or discuss the approach in committed forums. There is no cryptocurrency fee, and also the principles are transparent. When there were any drawbacks, it could be the UI of this site is much like gambling in Windows 95.

2. Academic Research

Darknet tools like Sci-Hub provide free access to thousands of academic documents, but these solutions are not necessarily legal. You are better off sticking with routine net resources like Google Scholar to stop from breaking intellectual property legislation. Late last year, the American Journal of Freestanding Research Psychology (AJFRP) became the first open and free Darknet academic journal. All academic papers have to be filed by the original writers. It remains to be seen whether AJFRP will grow to be a successful job or perhaps the very first of several darknet-based academic exchanges.

3. ProPublica

This American nonprofit news company has been the first Significant media outlet To make a dedicated presence on the darknet in 2016. ProPublica specializes in investigative public-interest journalism and has been the very first online-only source to win a Pulitzer Prize in 2010. The onion website provides anonymous access to people globally, such as readers in nations where journalism is closely censored.

"Everybody should Be Able to decide What Kinds of metadata that they Leave behind," ProPublica programmer Mike Tigas informed Wired. "We do not want anybody to know that you just came to us what you see."

4. SecureDrop

This open-minded entry system is widely used by journalists. Anonymously communicate with resources. SecureDrop does not record a submitter's IP address or some other browser info, just storing the time and date of messages. Forbes, The New

Yorker, The Washington Post and also Vice Media are only a few of many significant media outlets that use SecureDrop. A full record of embracing media outlets is available on the agency's surface site.

The U.S. government can also be experimentation with SecureDrop to possibly Accept anonymous vulnerability reports and collaborate with white hat hackers, per CyberScoop.

5. The CIA

Other agencies have embraced a presence on the darknet to promote anonymous Cooperation with resources. The U.S. Central Intelligence Agency (CIA) has an onion website using a"Contact Us" form. The website comprises a guarantee to"carefully safeguard all information you provide, including your individuality."

6. Tor Metrics

Tor Project Metrics includes a double presence around the surface net and darknet. It publishes anonymous information and analytics, providing insight to just how the Tor browser technology is currently utilized, and from whom. An academic study of Tor metrics demonstrated that 60 percent of Tor's use is for lawful purposes. Political censorship tops the list of why users download Tor for noncriminal purposes.

7. IIT Tunnels

The Illinois Institute of Technology campus at Chicago is Full of covert Tunnels, initially constructed for telecommunication access points, services entrances or steam vents. This elaborate underground community has inspired hundreds of student pranks and many more conspiracy theories. 1 darknet user committed to fully exploring these tunnels also has released his findings and photographs on the internet. While there is no guarantee the writer did not violate trespassing legislation, this darknet website is really clean entertainment.

8. Anonymous Email

There are lots of heavily encrypted email providers on the darknet. ProtonMail is one of the finest known. This end-to-end encrypted support was designed by MIT and CERN scientists also have an existence on the outside net. Like many other details of the darknet, an entirely anonymized email is neither great nor bad by itself. It is neutral, and there are absolutely legitimate usage cases. By way of instance, an individual may install ProtonMail to make a darknet baseball account.

9. Ad-Free Search

You will find darknet search engines, but they are mostly research jobs that Try to index onion websites. Nearly All the deep net remains inaccessible Through any way apart from wiki lists. Darknet search engines like DuckDuckGo exist to crawl the outside net when shielding Tor user anonymity. You won't find onion websites on DuckDuckGo, but you will Have the Ability to hunt without Advertisements.

10. Tor Kittenz

Tor Kittenz is a now-defunct Tor site that was literally Only a slideshow Of user-submitted cat images. The site looked just like a 1990s-style throwback, but it was a welcome respite from content that is darker on the deep net.

Is Your Darknet All Bad?

The darknet is not entirely prohibited action. There are some bright spots in Between offender marketplaces and hacker forums. Additionally, there are significant use cases for darknet solutions, like anonymous communication with intelligence bureaus or amusement. In the same way, the countless Tor users globally do not signify the darknet has hit the mainstream. Oftentimes, users download Tor to prevent censorship legislation or to just protect private data while surfing the outside net.

While there are wikis, forums and sites dedicated to indexing darknet Links, it is difficult to pin down precisely what is under the surface. The hidden web is not indexed by major search engines. The nearest we could come to knowing good versus bad on the darknet is through jobs like Hyperion Gray's data visualization channels. Aside from occasional bright places and valid usage instances, the sub-surface net is a cloudy place best left to danger intelligence specialists.

7 Ways that the Hidden World of the Darknet Is Evolving

The darknet Is not as concealed as it was. The seamy electronic underbelly of the world wide web, according to your sources, could be diminishing or entering the mainstream. All things considered, any savvy person can work out how to obtain a Tor browser and then utilize cryptocurrency.

Risks are definitely greater than for cybercriminals. Using the darknet To publicly market narcotics, stolen illegal or data services. The first Silk Road creator, Ross Ulbricht, has dropped appeals against a dual life sentence and 40 years for offenses of drug trafficking and money laundering under the top layer of the internet. Plus it's easy to feel that the darknet is not as funny as it was based on media stories. Narcotics traffickers are banning sales of their synthetic opioid fentanyl because of security concerns. Actually, Facebook has gone dim with an onion website obtained by 1 million Tor browser users every month.

Even though the darknet is much more heavily trafficked than ever, the conflict is not over. Authentic hazard intelligence found in hard-to-access corners of the internet, far away from important marketplaces and media reports. Hazards to the venture beneath the surface net are not shrinking. In reality, based on recent research, hidden dangers to your company are growing quickly.

7 Darknet Threat Trends to Keep an Eye On

Global law enforcement agencies are working with

coordinated Ability to close down darknet marketplaces. According to Bitcoin Magazine, the current shutdown of the dark website Wall Street Marketplace involved the concerted efforts of the German Federal Criminal Police, the Dutch National Police, Europol, Eurojust, and assorted U.S. government agencies, such as the FBI, IRS and DOJ. When these efforts are laudable, fresh marketplaces demonstrate criminal trade isn't so readily stopped.

"Instability is now kind of baked to the dark-web market encounter," Darknet specialist Emily Wilson told The New York Times. "People do not get quite as fearful by [raids] because they did the first couple of times."

Unpredictable changes and increased risks of prosecution aren't Enough to dissuade cybercriminals. More to the point, the most crucial enterprise risks operate deep underneath the surface.

1. The Darknet Is Over Tor

There is a Frequent misconception that the darknet is a phrase for sites Available with a Tor browser. But, there is more under the surface compared to .onion extensions.

"The' darknet,' in general, means it is a community or space Online That is not readily available to ordinary folks," said Andrei Barysevich of Recorded Future.

Barysevich noted that numerous criminal Websites, forums and communities predate The invention of Tor. Though a few of those hubs have proceeded into Tor, others stay online with different protocols like I2P, GNUnet or even Riffle.

2. Enterprise Threats Are Growing

It is a dangerous error to completely connect the darknet with Well-known dangers, like the selling of narcotics or script kiddies buying dispersed denial-of-service (DDoS) attacks as an agency. Between 2016 and 2019, there was a 20 percent gain in the number of darknet listings that have the potential to cause injury to associations, as per a recent academic analysis using Bromium. Growing dangers include:

Targeted malware;
Enterprise-specific DDoS providers;
Corporate information available; and
Brand-spoofing phishing tools.

The best cybercriminals will also be highly guarded. Seventy percent Of sellers that participated with academic investigators were just keen to communicate through personal channels.

3. Darknet Trends Mirror Enterprise Threats

Darknet hazard trends closely reflect the evolution of the enterprise hazard vector. 1 such example involves the recent development of whaling strikes. This past year, 13 percent of strikes examined by IBM X-Force Incident Response and Intelligence Services (IRIS) involved company email compromise (BEC) or whaling, based on this"2019 IBM X-Force Threat Intelligence Index Report." Access to company email accounts may be purchased if whalers can not purchase the credentials they want from credential retailers. The normal price of compromising a company email account is only $150, based on Digital Shadows.

4. Social Engineering Fodder Is Openly Exchanged

In 2019, there has been a disturbing tendency toward the sale of whole digital Identities belonging to people infected by malware, based on ZDNet. Each electronic profile comprises login credentials for internet banking, file sharing and social media. Web cookies, browser user-agent particulars, HTML5 canvas fingerprints and other information can also be included for a price ranging from $5 to $200.

Societal Engineering strikes are getting more concentrated. The most recent wave is immune to some kind of protection besides advanced behavioral analytics. This season has witnessed a rapid increase in direct extortion efforts against high-profile people, in addition to pretexting strikes where somebody assumes the identity of a trusted party. It is simple for threat celebrities to slide on a different likeness after buying a whole digital identity in 1 transaction.

5. Network Access Could Be Bought and Sold

The Array of services Which Can Be bought is wide, and hazard actors Prepared to cover immediate access can have it. According to the preceding academic analysis by Bromium, researchers have been provided backdoors into corporate networks -- through sellers refused to supply details on such backdoors with no significant upfront fee. At least 60 percent of non-sellers openly offered entry to over 10 high-profile company networks through remote access Trojans (RATs), exploits and keyloggers.

6. Your Intellectual Property May Be for Sale

The darknet is a sanctuary for the exchange of business trade secrets and intellectual property. Additionally, it is a hangout for malicious insiders that provide access to trade secrets. Forums even occasionally host talks about business workers likely to be exposed to extortion efforts. When the investigators supporting the Bromium report requested one seller about gaining community access to three major businesses, they found it was both economical and effortless. 1 darknet seller supplied"accessibility to the CEO" or to"get whatever we wanted out of their servers" for charges which varied from $1,000--$15,000.

In case your intellectual property has been compromised or you are employing a Malicious insider, it is difficult to tell because many strategies to darknet hazard tracking focus on keywords or business alarms.

7. Risks Hide at the Recesses of the Darknet

Nearly All cybercriminals and the very sophisticated threat

actors Operate outside perspective. The corners of this darknet contain criminal social networks, internet forums and password-protected communities. These haunts are probably even vaguer than you believe.

The Number of inbound hyperlinks to internet communities may be Utilized as one step of accessibility. Popular surface sites might have countless linking domain names. Recorded Future recently conducted an investigation of "top-tier criminal websites using significant barriers to entry and also a high amount of obscurity." These sites had a mean of 8.7 inbound hyperlinks, using a maximum number of 15 inbound hyperlinks. The strangest websites contain the most precious threat intelligence.

The Darknet Is Simply Shrinking Away In The Surface

The Most Critical risks to the enterprise function from the hidden corners Of the internet. Cybercrime collectives and thoroughly skilled hackers discuss password-protected platforms, invitation-only forums and personal messaging programs. Digital communities with large barriers to entry are best for communicating between cybercrime collectives or even the open move of corporate intellectual property.

Since the darknet slides further beneath the surface, it is time for the Enterprise to appear deeper than surface-level cyberthreat intellect . The capacity to track, name and identify risks requires organizations to utilize hazard intelligence flows that reach to the corners of their hidden web. Darknet information is a workable intelligence resource, but only as long as your information accessibility is as wide-reaching and fast to evolve because of cybercriminals.

The Darknet and Deep Web

In this Era of developing technologies, we hope the net. We hope it with making protected payments, keeping our health care history and sharing private photographs with family members and friends. We hope a site once it asserts our advice is protected from intruders and when our data is submitted individually, it's only ours to view.

But, Once data is submitted, sent, or clicked, it's public. Hackers can creep into these allegedly private portal sites and extract details.

The vast Internet includes 3 layers. The initial layer is public, comprising websites we regularly use like Facebook, Twitter, Amazon and LinkedIn. This coating makes up just 4% of the full Internet.

What's Another 96 percent? The deep net along with the darknet. The deep net, the next coating, is a system where information is stored in databases that are inaccessible. The darknet is that the third largest, deeper layer of the Web by which hackers congregate and ease meetings that are illegal. Clients whose information is broken don't have access to this darknet.

Tor (originally short for The Onion Router) started life as a U.S. Navy job for anonymous online action but is now employed by a broad assortment of classes, including the army, journalists, bloggers, activists and, yes, offenders. Tor makes communications more difficult to follow through traffic investigation by routing Internet action through a collection of network nodes, each ignorant of the entire path from beginning to finish. The trade-off for greater safety is a slower rate.

To browse The darknet, we utilize a browser which allows us to get .onion websites with telephone browsers such as:

Tor Browser
TAILS

Onion Browser

Or, Sites like"Tor2Web" and"Onion2web" may be used, allowing users to readily access .onion websites on browsers such as Google Chrome. As simple as this could be, it ensures that your IP address is vulnerable -- and whenever this occurs, you are open to all kinds of attacks from hackers.

Here are Some actions to shield your personal computer:

After users browse the darknet, it opens up their pc to potential scans and malware which could compromise their system. Don't browse the darknet from a computer onto your work system. Utilize a computer that you're inclined to reconstruct, and utilize a VPN to secure your network link. I would also recommend using applications that can guard your pc against any changes like:

Deep Freeze

Sandboxie

SmartShield

SysFreezer

Be safe and don't allow any Macros or scripts on a .onion

website

Don't download files off untrusted or unknown websites.

Don't purchase anything on the darknet since there are a lot of scams. Buyers may never hear from the vendor, and what exactly you're buying could be prohibited.

Be cautious of what you might discover on the darknet since it might be associated with something illegal -- weapons, drugs, hackers, porn and classified information. You might need to report to the government that which you find and clarify what you're doing. Additional, nearly all dark web trades use cryptocurrencies such as Bitcoins; therefore it is entirely untraceable, and a refund is generally from the question.

Don't make enemies or friends on the darknet; messing with a hacker has the potential to mess up your life.

You can utilize services which can search for you personally, or Permit You to look in a secure way, such as Harris company's TORNADO.TM

What are Some motives to look for the darknet? There might be business data that could be on the darknet today, for example, username and passwords, network maps, and other private information that could be debatable. Once users become proficient at hunting the darknet, they could produce a seed file. A seed file is preserved internally by businesses. Locating these on the darknet is an indication that the business was compromised.

Dark Internet Links To Get Darknet Markets

This is a thickness list of profound net marketplaces you can use to buy or sell different kinds of services and goods. I update the list regularly so you could discover all active marketplace places links at the same location without wasting time. There are tons of items that you want to remember while purchasing or selling goods/services in darknet markets such as constantly utilize 2FA login, just trusted market location, confirmed buyer and vendor, etc..

If You're new to the dim net, please check the way to Access darknet with a complete privacy manual.

Care : Tor Browser does not offer complete anonymity. So first operate NordVPN and join with Onion Over VPN Server then start Tor Browser. Today you're fully protected and prepared to research darknet markets.

6ngvt5ueyjyo62zx -- Darkweb Marketplace -- Empire Market -- Recently established market that's a replica of Alphabay

Marketplace, searching alternative shop on Alphabay, you might attempt Empire marketplace, Like any other dark web marketplace, where consumers can also deal lawful or prohibited things (Medication, Digital Products, Games, Virus, Hacking service, Hosting and etc). Empire market takes a commission in several crypto coins such as BTC, BCH, LTC, XMR. They also aim to include new crypto coins within this shop.

grymktgwyxq3sikl -- Darknet Marketplace -- Grey Market is a market both for Buyers and Sellers. Buyers can purchase from over 700 listings around the market in a variety of categories like E-books, Software, Weed, Stimulants, Seeds etc.. While Vendors can market these products to get a vendor-bond of USD $99.00 plus a cost of 5%-3% on every sale (depends upon seller levels). Payment manners: BTC and XMR. Safety: Escrow/ Wallet-less deposits. PGP available also.

samsaraccrn2jmin -- Darknet Markets -- Samsara Market -- This can be the most reliable darknet marketplace, which have more than one Lakh recorded items, services or products and these are associated with Medicines, Digital Goods, Services, Electronics, Carding, Hacking, Porns Accounts, Counterfeit, Malware, Virus, Harness and a whole lot more. Since from few months, fantasy market getting his commission in three hot cryptocurrencies (Bitcoins, Bitcoin Cash, Monero). For safety reasons it's possible to place 2FA in your account by PGP Key.

berlusconifsfwkp -- Darknet Marketplace -- Two principal facets of any DNM comprise its"Products", and"Security Characteristics ". Products available on Berlusconi marketplace include everything and anything from Medicines, Carded things, Jewellery, Gold etc.. Security features include 2-Factor authentication via PGP, Escrow and Multisig for safer trade and transactions, and PIN for Withdrawal and refund-address changes. Bitcoin, Litecoin as well as Monero approved as payment manners. It can be retrieved only after registrations.

darknet4rbfizlg53dwc5lt5hj4mewcgltubcpvrfpvjavm64inaf3a d -- Darknet Market -- DarkMarket is a Darknet Market selling Medicines, Guides, Services, Jewellery, Carded Things, Malware and many other Darknet Products. Accepts Vendors to get USD $99.00 Vendor charge. Accepts payments through Bitcoin and Monero. 2-FA, PGP Encryption, Escrow and Mnemonic signal accessible. Boasts 14,000+ goods, and 621 Vendors as of now.

wallstyizjhkrvmj -- Darkweb Marketplace -- WallStreet

Marketplace (Exit Scam)- I'm discovering Wallstreet marketplace functionality because of the few months and detect today lot's of individuals favor Wallstreet markets for producing trades on the dark net. Now, this shadowy net market has over 10000+ records that are still growing day daily. If you're interested in finding other darknet markets then this is your shop for you.

Azworldjqhsr4pd5 -- Darkweb Marketplace -- [A-Z Earth] Trade (Scammer) -- A Darknet Marketplace that is a card along with Socks5 checker; also contains a stock of over 1116+ person listings.

Additionally boasts an auto-shop That's packed with Cards, PayPal accounts, RDPs and Socks5. Another section of this Darknet Market sells things related to Fraud, Guides, Exploits, Hacking, Tutorials, SQL shots etc..

It does enable individual users vending on the stage for USD $60.00 (refundable). Offers 2-Fa, accounts retrieval duration, private expression, Escrow and PIN. Payment may only be made utilizing Bitcoins.

valhallaxmn3fydu -- Darknet Markets -- Valhalla Darkweb Market: This market is trusted, Everyday with over thousands of consumers to Valhalla. In this dark net sites, you can get over 25K+ recorded items, which can be associated with Medicines, Body Building, Cannabis climbing, mushroom growing, Production/distribution, paraphernalia, electronic objects, self-defense, services, classifieds.

Notice: If You Would like to purchase drugs afterward Valhalla darkweb marketplace can Provide you the best things.

tochka3evlj3sxdv -- Darknet Markets -- Tochka Darkweb Market: In case you're searching another darknet market options, then Tochka marketplace will be able to assist you. Here you can find goods associated with Medications, Digital Goods, Prescription, Guides and Tutorials, Software, Services, Others, Steroids. However, this market has restricted items, recorded items amount 400+.

hky3mzk3jtmd4zt4 -- Berlusconi Market

Here you can get everything from Fraud, Drugs & Chemicals, Guides & Tutorials, Counterfeit products, electronic products, Jewels & Gold, Weapons, Carded items, to applications and malware as well as a lot of other stuff. When you register, you can get recorded items in this darknet market.

You do not have to deposit Bitcoins, you may use their hardened bitcoin escrow. If you would like to understand more about Berlusconi Market, it is possible to navigate the cited onion connection.

weasylartw55noh2 -- Weasyl

This market is devoted to the artwork gallery. Weasyl supplies a center to artists, writers to discuss their work with different musicians and lovers. Artist also lists their gallery for sale. If you're thinking about purchasing an original gallery out of musicians, it is possible to see a given onion connection. It's different from many other darknet markets.

un62d2ywi33bho53 -- UnderMarket (Scammer)

Here You'll get Carding, Counterfeit Money, Medicines, Electronics products, and present Cards, PayPal Accounts, along with other providers. They do not sell things themselves. The most important intention of UnderMarket is supplying Multisig Escrow support together with a listing of vendors with products and testimonials. To learn more about UnderMarket, it is possible to have a look at deep links.

vnjzhvm5gkctyldn -- SearchOpenBazaar

SearchOpenBazaar is a recently established market. Its user interface is quite organized. Here you'll discover any great with selected accepted currents and user score. SearchOpenBazaar delivers physical products, electronic products, and other providers. Here it is possible to also deal in mature content. Supported monies are Bitcoin, Bitcoin Cash, ZCash. It supplies shipping services globally. Presently, it's 34K things available for sale.

greenroxwc5po3ab -- Green Road

Green Road is devoted to medication. Green Road provides Cannabis, Depressants, Empathogens, Opiates, Pharmacy, Psychedelics, and Stimulants. Presently, Green Road contains 10 million medications. You are able to navigate this market after enrollment only. If you're interested in finding dark links that deal with drugs, then you are able to think about this one as it's devoted to only medication. Prior to making an order together, check testimonials about Green Road in additional shadowy forums.

cards5yvy44gucvo -- Plastic Marketplace

Plastic Marketplace is your biggest carding shop on the shadowy net. It provides just Assessed and legitimate balances, cards or counterfeits, PayPal. If you would like to sell hacked accounts and dumps frequently, you can get in touch with them. Supported money for buying and selling is Bitcoin. Plastic Marketplace also supplies shipping services globally as with other darknet markets.

hydraruzxpnew4af -- HYDRA

Hydra is in the Russian language, so in the Event That You know Russian believe this Otherwise proceed to next. Hydra bargains in Marijuana, Stimulators, Eyforetics, Psychedelics, Entheogens, Ecstasy, Dissociatives, Opiates, Chemical reagents / / Constructors, Pharmacy, SSH, VPN, Digital products, Records, Cards, SIM, Design and images, Outdoor advertisements, Counterfeit cash, Instruments and gear, Anabolics / Steroids, Partnership and Franchise, occupation along with others. Every class has great quantities of goods to select from. If you're interested in finding the Russian darknet marketplace then it is possible to have a look at onion link to learn more about Hydra.

l3pwaatzhgswqur3 -- Darknet Markets/French -- DarkShop: According to site status, this can be a french based darknet market, where you could deal with multiple goods. If you're searching for some curry choice, then these shadowy net links will be able to assist you.

leomarketjdridoo -- Darknet Markets -- House of Lions: This dark net links encourage 2FA authentication and support Escrow support. Both may help you for a safe deal on this market. House of Lion's dark net marketplace has over 2000 set items and here accessible classes are Drugs, weapons, services, fraud Related, Guides & Tutorials, Counterfeit Items, Additional Listings.

reloadxnkwi5nsbg -- Darknet Markets -- Silk Road 3: Everybody knows about Silk street dark website, after closed down silk street 1, silk street two, today we've got silk street 3. However, I believe that is trustable in accordance with silk street 2 or 1. Like other dim web marketplaces this website additionally encourages 2FA authentication and Escrow. But the stage isn't user-friendly.

(Seized) pwoah7foa6au2pul -- Darknet Markets -- Alphabay Darknet Market: Alphabay Is the most reliable and largest darkweb sector. This site has over 250000+ recorded items that are enormous. Here you Can Purchase Fraud, Drugs & Chemicals, Guide & Tutorials, Counterfeit Things, Digital Products, Weapons, Carded Things, Services, Other Listings, Software & Malware, Security & Hostings.

(Seized) hansamkt2rr6nfg3 -- Darknet Markets -- Hansa Market: This shadowy net markets Provide all kind product-related provider, here it is possible to purchase a solution and also can record your product for sale. This darkweb website is having more than one Lakh recorded items associated with counterfeit, tutorials, hacking, firearms, weapons, and much more.

acropol4ti6ytzeh -- Darknet Markets -- Acropolis Markets: This darknet marketplace also reliable and a lot of consumers used this market, but these dim sites don't have many recorded products. Here you are able to locate Bitcoin Security, Medicines, E-books, Others, Services categories.

acropol4ti6ytzeh -- Darknet Markets -- Acropolis: This is just another darkneT marketplace, which has largely drugs associated recorded items, but once I checked this website then the market simply has approx 500 + recorded objects. From

500 only drugs class have 440+ things.

udujmgcoqw6o4cp4 -- Darknet Markets -- UnderGround: Another very best dark online marketplace link for most significant services, If you're searching any very best choice for alpha bay or fantasy marketplace, you might like underground. In accordance with the market here there is Finance (PayPal Accounts, Prepaid Cards), Digital (Sport Console, Tablets, Computers, Phones), Document(Driver License, ID Cards, Passport, Diploma), Risk (Computer Virus, Weapons, Hackers), Extra(Medicine, Humen Organs, Professional Killers) associated Company, You can but those kind listed products into affordable BTC price.

lnkfzecnslxo6jqc -- Darknet Market Link -- Rapture

On the lookout to get darknet market connection on the deep net? Rapture is the place that you may love to research. Here you can get Barbiturates, Benzos, Cannabis, Digital Goods, Dissociatives, Ecstasy, Opioids, Prescription, Psychedelics, RCs, Steroids, Stimulants, and Weight loss pills. They've recorded their top 10 sellers on their home page. However, to get this fantasy marketplace content, you will need to make an account. When you sign up, you can check pricing information, accessible products and seller details. You may just see given onion-like to find out more about Rapture.

cavetord6bosm3sl -- Dark Social Network -- Cave Tor

Cave Tor is over darknet marketplace as the title indicates. Shop segment is Split into 5 classes drug store, electronic store, fiscal services, other store and solutions. Here you can acquire many products linked to different store categories. Cave Tor has communities and forums too. If you would like to share things with other community members then you may register here to join. Different segments of Cave Tor are information, direct, escrow, photographs, blogs, Q&A, individuals and wiki links Tor. For the appropriate loading of the site, you will need to enable JavaScript that isn't advised on deep internet.

blackmarthw3vp7a -- BlackMarket

If You're Looking for a Russian market on the deep web, then BlackMarket can be a great selection for you. If you do not know Russian speech, avoid this. Here you'll find 10000+ goods that are linked to classes including medications, hacking, weapons, fake documents and much more. Even a few traders offer delivery worldwide.

o3cvx3oxareo7aop -- The Open Road

To get listed items in The Open Road, then you have to make an account. As my personal experience, I did not find any item here after enrolling. Should they upgrade in the future, I'm happy to upgrade. Guidelines and standards are given in your home page. I am not positive when they have something or not.

tochka3evlj3sxdv -- Tochka Free Market

Tochka is among the earliest darkent markets, based in 2015. Supported Crypto monies are Bitcoin, Bitcoin money & Ethereum. Support can be found in a variety of languages. To learn more about recorded items at Tochka, you want to make an account.

midcity7ccxtrzhn -- Midland City

Midland city Provides digital products, including PayPal cards, accounts, and pornography Life accounts of digitalplayground.com. Mdiland city also deals in medications such as Benzos, Cannabis, Dissociatives, Ecstasy, and Opioids. Products are somewhat less as compared to additional darknet markets. The shipping service is global. Shipping days are Monday, Wednesday and Friday. To find out more, you are able to assess their about us page and you have any questions then you may contact us and ask your own query.

Email & Chat Dark Internet Links

Searching for deep links that provide the facility to make anonyms mails and performing chat? Now I have put together a listing of anonymous and chat email darknet site hyperlinks.

I update this listing regularly to supply you with busy tor links. Since locating Onion links aren't easy as they're concealed and lots of instances Tor search engines are likewise not cable to index them.

Some email providers provide superior services. Premium services are Always best because they're more protected and include a few innovative capabilities.

Care : If You're exploring dark net with Tor browser just then you aren't safe. Tor Browser does not supply you with complete anonymity and security. So consistently use premium VPN support, if you ask my proposal, I'll urge NordVPN because they've committed Onion More than VPN Servers, and their rate can also be high, and they overcome their opponents in several capabilities.

As Soon as You have NordVPN installed in your pc, always follow below hints to make a safe atmosphere.

Close all active programs on your PC.

Run NordVPN Software and join Onion Over VPN server.

Start Tor Browser and disable javascript.

Now You're ready to explore dark net with an Excess layer of anonymity and encryption. With dual-layer of safety, it's not possible to follow you.

Let us begin with all the chat and anonymous email hyperlinks.

Ozon3kdtlr6gtzjn -- Mail -- O3mail

O3mail also provides anonymous email support. However, to utilize O3mail Assistance, you need to enable JavaScript on your Tor Browser setting that isn't great for a concealed user.

scryptmaildniwm6 -- Emails -- Scryptmail

If solitude is a significant consideration and looking for a superior anonymous email Service supplier, then it is possible to check this dark link. In addition, they provide 7-day trial so that I will recommend you prior to purchasing the first move with 7-day trial after which determine it is best or will need to search for additional alternative deep links.

bitmailendavkbec -- Email -- Bitmessage Mail Gateway

This dark link provides you a facility to attach Bitmessage with Mail With no program. Bitmessage Network isn't hard to use like Mail now. Utilizing given onion connection, you may produce private Bitmessage speech, readily send and receive emails from/to other email addresses. Some wonderful characteristics of this dark link are Vehicle responder, Car forwarder, broadcasting, two-car signatures and a lot more. The finest thing about this anonymous email service supplier is it is totally free.

it.louhlbgyupgktsw7 -- Deep Web Emails -- Onion Mail

Onion Mail is just another operating anonymous email

service supplier at a concealed web. To make a fresh Onion Mail accounts, you will need to click Download choice and after that you'll become aware of a different window with a message"To make a new OnionMail accounts click HERE". To find out more regarding Onion Mail attributes and solutions, please see mention Tor URL.

nzh3fv6jc6jskki3 -- Communication Tools -- Riseup

Riseup is much more than the anonymous email service provider. It supplies you with several safe communication tools for people that are focusing on liberatory social change. They provide two kind accounts is Riseup Red and next is Riseup Black. Riseup crimson balances are for traditional services comprises Mail, Chat and VPN while Riseup black balances are for new providers that require Bitmask applications. Some tutorials and resources will also be available for more secure communication. For better comprehension, it is possible to check the site yourself.

clgs64523yi2bkhz -- Emails -- Mailpile

Mailpile is an email client that protects your privacy and provides personal Communicating online. Some wonderful attributes of Mailpile are Strong tagging & search, quick and responsive, Storing emails on apparatus you restrain, OpenPGP signatures and encryption, zero advertisements and self-hosted etc.. It is totally free and open source applications. At the site segment, you'll come across some excellent stuff. For more information visit this dark link yourself. I believe they're offering many incredible features like a top anonymous email service provider. In case you choose to go for this profound web email service supplier link, do not forget to talk about your expertise with us.

doggyfipznipbaia -- Chat/Email -- CryptoDog

Want to Go over about some issues with other looking finest Personal chat server for this goal? Then you can consider CryptoDog. Always keep 1 thing in your mind as you're talking something at deep internet, never share any personal information with any penis. To utilize this, you want to enable JavaScript. Since Cryptodog use JavaScript for messaging and encryption. Go and check this profound link.

campfireagz2uf22 -- Chat/Email -- The Campfire

The Campfire is following choice for Chat/Email deep links.

To learn more about the Campfire features, You Have to navigate the above-given connection yourself because I did not know it much once I assessed. If you know what they are offering, Don't hesitate to talk with us. I'm happy to upgrade your own expertise here.

r2j4xiyckibnyd45 -- Tor Chat Room -- BoyChat

BoyChat is a boylove message board for boy fans That Are Looking for a boy Love profound internet forum link for discussion and chat. In case it interests you, then see over the mentioned dark link. For your safety and comfort, original assess rules before involvement in dialogue. Rules link can be obtained in addition to the page. For actual time plus one-liner, you may use The Treehouse alternative. If you would like to go over about alluring and present topics, then contemplate the OtherChat alternative.

4fvfamdpoulu2nms -- Chat -- Lucky Eddie's Home

Lucky Eddie's Home offers you two solutions: LE CHAT Chat-Script and second is Batch Up! File Uploader. If you're seeking something to establish your webchat, then you're likely to enjoy LE Chat Script. Along with using a File uploader, it is possible to your uploading work simpler. This Uploader script works nicely with Windows. In case you have any confusion about this profound link, read once yourself.

Ozon3kdtlr6gtzjn -- Mail -- Roundcube: that shadowy net Website also offers anonymous email support; I really don't understand how this website work, but if you're searching sigaint.org choice, hope this might help you.

Cwu7eglxcabwttzf -- Mail -- Confident Mail: this Website Also provides email support; if you're still searching various other options, then you may try out this website.

Eozm6j6i4mmme2p5 -- Mail -- MailCity: This Website provides Permanent, mobile email service that means that you don't have to modify your speech from time to time.

Sinbox4irsyaauzo -- Mail -- Sinbox: still appearing the Deep internet email sites then check out sinbox, this will be the predicated on the multi-layered encrypted procedure. For Security purposes, when you make an account on Sinbox dark net email website, the time you have one special viewing secrets, and you'll be able to save yourself this crucial locally anywhere to your system. If you would like to log in your email accounts, then you want to provide that special viewing essential, if the key will be verified, then your account will be displayed on the screen.

iwab42vsaivtzkf5 -- Communication Tool -- Anonymous Says

Anonymous Says enable you to post messages. If You Would like to post something Secretly or without showing identity, then this dim net link will be able to assist you. It's possible to post legal content just as they state links of prohibited material, spam and doxing aren't permitted.

Grrmailb3fxpjbwm -- Mail -- TorGuerrillaMail -- Disposable Temporary E-Mail Speech

TorGuerrilaMail enables you to create a temporary email address within seconds. Registration isn't required. Email address continues 60 mins. If you're interested in finding a dark web site in order to create bogus email addresses to prevent spam in your principal email, then head to TorGuerrillaMail onion connection. To utilize all attributes, you have to enable Javascript. That is the thing that I do not connect about TorGuerrillaMail.

csclonezdiriab5k -- Chat -- CS Clone

CS Clone offers immediate multi-room chat service at no cost. You can use this Room chat support without registration. Here you can make your own space or may join a space for chatting and talking within seconds. Here you are able to invite additional people also to explore any specific topic. It is possible to take advantage of this area chat server support at cellular too. A few other characteristics of CS Clone really are a secure personal message, auto-scrolling, embedded pictures, super muffle, quoting a person, sorting, and audio notifications etc..

Qj3m7wxqk4pfqwob -- Chat -- MadIRC Chat waiter

MadIRC Chat host is just another Wonderful anonymous conversation server in this listing of .onion links. Here you do not need to make an account to utilize the chat server center. To utilize this, you want to pick any arbitrary username/channel title and click the start button. When the link has been established, you may directly share it with the chat host's associates.

infantilefb6ovh4 -- Chat -- Infantile

Infantile offers amazing characteristics compared to other chat server dim web Websites. Here you do not need to follow some rules. Infantile is a featured oriented XMPP communication machine. Additionally, it has an IRC server that you may use after enrollment. In addition, it supplies you IMAP/POP3 email accounts for which you have to pay $10 a month. If you discover Infantile intriguing, you may see the website onion link for more information.

danschatjr7qbwip -- Chat -- Daniel's Chat

Daniel's conversation is following mention for discussion server dark links. It offers you a Chatting center. Here you can join a chat room and talk with other people. You have to adhere to all offered guidelines by site admin to utilize this site. This site provides some other darknet providers pumpkin hyperlinks, and you'll discover in the sidebar.

onionirczesfffux -- Chat Server Tutorial -- Onionnet IRC Hideout

Here you may learn about IRC network-based chat server. This tor Connection Does not provide chatting and email service but it brings several helpful information about Hexchat, Pidgin, weechat, irssi, mirc.

etatl6umgbmtv27 -- Chat -- Chat with Strangers

This tor link enables you to talk with strangers along with your pals. It's very User friendly. An individual can use it effortlessly. If you would like to talk to your friends, click Chat with buddy choice, you'll find a link that you will need to send your buddy to talk with him/her. This profound site supports 4 languages. It gives an exceptional feature, unlike other shadowy links in the listing. You do not need to make an account to utilize this site.

Cockmailwwfvrtqj -- Mail -- Cock.li -- it's email With cocks: see this website and make your accounts and share your comments with us, the way to website work and your expertise. Since I really don't have my account on this website, that is why I do not understand how this dim net hyperlinks function.

Torbox3uiot6wchz -- Mail -- TorBox: Are you currently appearing fully Torbox service anonymous email support then it is possible to attempt torbox since you can just send or get messages into torbox from tor network. You are able to send messages by people's net.

344c6kbnjnljjzlz -- Mail -- VFEmail: Still searching some fantastic email support then attempt this dark web hyperlinks, which offer numerous packages that you may select based on your selection and requirement.

Mail2get4idcbfwe -- Mail -- Mail2tor: Another popular email support that also focusing on anonymous surroundings, Largely deep web user employed Mail2tor email services. This Is Totally free email support not accepting any charge for Certain premium plans

Dhbzkbw3ngxxt56q -- Mail -- SimplePM: that can be time Base email support means whenever you stop by this website, then it is possible to make a new inbox for you. If you would like to see your preceding tune, then you will need to submit a bookmark URL.

vola7ileiax4ueow -- Chat/Email -- Volatile

Next select in the listing of dim links for chat/email is Volatile. Volatile Provides chat, Git, Email & XMPP and a lot more services. I'm not able to determine how it functions.

Assess once your self and if you realize this dark site functioning, please write to us too. I really could share the same with my own readers.

cadamailgxsy6ykq -- Email -- Cicada Mail

Cicada Mail is just another email service provider at a dim net. To know what exactly they're providing, you have to see given onion yourself. Before clicking entering, read attentively their duration of services, cookie and privacy policy that are written in their own homepage.

Oxicsiwet42jw4h4 -- Mail -- Bitmaila: This Dark link also offer email support, I believe that is recently launched email support that provides 500 MB mail space and cost will be $0.60 for life.

mswmailgcjbye4sc -- Chat/Email -- My Secrete World: According to this website, this will be the neighborhood based on security, liberty, cooperation and anonymity. This website supplies you with an anonymous chat platform where you are able to ask anything anonymously.

pmasonkivrbmjlkv -- Emails -- P-Mail fearr

P-mail Fearr is supplying anonymous email support in dark net from 2017. Also enable you to include smtp.pmail.i2p / pop.pmail.i2p. When you enroll at this dark link, you may able to learn more about them.

jitjatxmemcaaadp -- Chat/Email -- JitJat

JitJat is your next selection for anonymous immediate messaging. You can Message, talk and discuss anything with JitJat members anonymously. If you're looking best dark net links for anonymous messaging, research this dark link after.

Dark Internet Links for Services

Here's an ultimate Collection of dim links That Offer services such as Hitman Service, UK Passport support; US fake driving permit support, USA citizenship support, programming job service and a lot more.

Therefore, if you're searching for such kind solutions, then have a look at the below section.

Caution: If you're browsing deep first time, then check out this information about getting dark web anonymous.

Anonymity is a significant concern whilst surfing deep web/dark net, so first operate your NordVPN and choose Onion Over VPN server, after the link is established then launch Tor Browser and do not forget to disable JavaScript. This manner, you include one additional layer of anonymity and encryption. Today nobody can trace you, in case they do they will find VPN IP, not your actual IP.

Notice: I'm sharing this information for instructional purposes only. Therefore, if you're going to these dark links, you're only responsible for any injury.

57f23hcybjqj4ime -- Service -- setThemFree: Now I discovered This profound internet site, and this really is a self-hosted website, which admin name is Yury Bulka, " I do not understand what kind service here it is possible to get, expect you may find.

kobrabd77ppgjd2r -- Service/Hacker -- Scott Arciszewski: This really is a self-explanatory site, here you'll get some fantastic items advice. Also, by this website that you can employ Scott for your programming undertaking. Services that you'll be able to get my Scott PHP, celebration, javascript with jQuery, HTML5, CSS3 and Java.

apfrontcaqoorlrkclifojs3fjp4wnqxvzzwsgpbzoqc4r7knvwakiy
d -- Antipuritansky Front

This dark website is devoted to sexual liberty, contrary to sexual violence. Here you'll see an enormous group of PDFs. It is possible to download these PDFs simply by clicking on the hyperlink.

estbdbp22h6ywcj5 -- Kabul War Diary

Here you can read about 75,000 key US army reports covering the war in Afghanistan. Here you may read content by Type, Category and date. If you're interested in reading about key documents, then it is possible to see this website in the listing of dim links.

ypyqkvgecfzq6mne -- Fabio Casi Doxed

This is the private blog of Fabio Casi. He shares some info about him and his Buddy in his website.

grams7enufi7jmdl -- Service -- Helix -- Grams: Much like information desk that is website also a part of Grams website, but this section also offers exceptional information exactly like data desk. In accordance with the segment, you can wash your bitcoins, in case you've got some trouble relevant bitcoins and would like to clean your bitcoin status afterward helix will be able to assist you. But before you have to understand a few additional pieces of information. Minimum BTC 0.02 BTC takes for the apparent procedure and his accepting fee 2.5percent for this particular procedure. Notice: I believe 2.5percent is enormous.

grams7enufi7jmdl -- Service -- Helix Light -- Grams: Hilix light also provide the same service exactly like Helix, for more info check helix services.

grams7enufi7jmdl -- Service -- Flow -- Grams: Same as preceding two lists, this segment also sub a part of Grams Dark Internet SEarch Engine, As stated by the dark links, if you would like to create any rememberable link then you may try out this website. For instance: you know all dark links are into encoded form, which can be rememberable but should you wish to try to remember these kind profound internet sites name, then you're able to create his title brief hyperlinks, which you may remember easily.

Lxhbgl43362zhmoc -- Employ A Hitman -- Hitman Guru -- If you're searching hitman service on the heavy web and would like to employ any individual for such kind service afterward I discovered one dim link which provides Hit on the blood, Raped, shot dead, torture, murdered, bone fracture, auto on fire and so forth.

Dark Internet Links For Hacking

If You're interested in hacking and Appearing active deep links for Recognizing about hacking suggestions, hacking services supplied by deep hackers and web groups too, then you'll really like to research the below collection.

A lot of actions are done on a deep net associated with hacking every day. Below I'm sharing several working dark links for hacking services and hacking tutorials.

Caution: Surfing shadowy net with Tor Browser Isn't safe. Consistently use Premium VPN Service using Tor Browser. Personally, I utilize NordVPN because they've committed Onion Over VPN Server plus they defeat other VPNs in several capabilities. NordVPN will help you in developing a complete protected and secure environment using an innovative encryption and anonymity layer.

Follow below steps consistently While surfing heavy hacking links.

First of close all working programs on your PC.

Start NordVPN and join Onion Over Server.

If the link was established, then launch Tor Browser. And also make sure the version that you're employing is the newest Tor Version.

Now all is completed and you're prepared to see given onion hyperlinks.

Notice: I'm sharing these hackings hyperlinks for instruction purposes only. If you do any action, I'm not responsible for any injury or damage. It's your personal responsibility and danger.

huomyxhpzx6mw74e6jfxtj5kmxov6wdmc62ylk6oc7feht5gnt uawaqd -- Rent A Hacker -- Hacker'sBay -- This is Darknet hacker community that provides hacking service on the deep internet, They offer services in PC Hacking, Social Media Hacking, Emails Hacking, DDoS Attacks, Website Hacking and a whole lot more. However they provide his commission based on solutions. For instance -- Based on his site, If a consumer needs social websites to account hacking such as Facebook, Twitter, Instagram then they will cost $350 to $700. For additional pricing detail, please investigate the listed link.

ytteyiazq2xyazjws45lxjpqie5krxdcoe4nr5vysldu54olnbtrg5qd -- Hire a Hacker -- Pseudo Harmer Hacker Searching for Hacking services on the Dark net? Hacker Pseudo Harmer offers precisely that. Unlike various other groups, they don't have a"no go" list. So they likely will hack any and everything so long as the price is correct.

Thus far, they have enlisted Cell phones, E-mails, Social Networking accounts and Numerous databases as their areas of experience. Claim delivery prior deadline. Orders have to be set manually. Prices also vary for every job.

vscvkdcnjpwkdumrrnxsfhmx5shkztqzehnkvelpfrzj7sqkra7bcj id -- Employ Hacker -- You can purchase Hacking-related providers from Pundit Hackers' Group. It is not a"Darknet Market" per se, but contains similar purposes. Is not individually-owned either entirely is a"set of hackers". It does not let"sellers" and is just supposed to market their particular services. All and any hacking tasks are approved. E-mail is the only mode of communicating/placing orders out there.

Wdnqg3ehh3hvalpe -- Hacking -- Keys open doors: This really is Really correct, keys open doors When I assess this dark net links standing, I don't understand. These dark net sites are offering when you stop by this website hope you'll find something great for you.

Timaq4ygg2iegci7 -- Hacking -- Txtorcon: I Really like that Library, that relies on twisted centered Python, even if you would like to understand real-time info regarding your tor like as circuit, flow, logging hidden providers, link to conducting Tor circuit and a whole lot more. Total information check this shadowy links.

hackcanl2o4lvmnv -- Hacking -- Hack Canads: These shadowy sites have a sufficient quantity of info when you attempt to click on the specified homepage; every homepage connection have a large quantity of information. HackCanada includes hacking, hacking, phreaking, payphones, Scams & Rip-Off, FreeDomination, E-Zines, Other Materials and Canadian Links.

Pmwdzvbyvnmwobk5 -- Service/Hacking -- Barmlab: that Darkweb website is suggested to Prague non-profit company that runs hackerspace. Would you need to attend his most recent event then have a look at this website updates regularly?

hackharhoaw3yk5q -- Service/Hacker -- Hacker for Hire: Do You've got some task for which you're looking for a hacker, and would like to finish your job then hacker for hire can supply you that kind support. Hacker for Hire can help you in Hacking, Social Networking dangers, Computer spying and surveillance Eliminate a connection, Find missing people, Background checks, SSN Trace, Online Dating Scams, Cyberbully & Cyber Stalked, Computer security training, Cyber Extortion, Dating, Tracking, Password and Cyber Fraud.

6dvj6v5imhny3anf -- Cyber-Guerrilla

If You Would like to learn about hacking and searching a place at deep internet then this Dark website can be an excellent selection for you. A lot of members are busy here with hacking abilities; You can visit this site and place your query to get the answer from hackers. It's possible to learn from older thread too that are about hacking. Don't hesitate to talk about your expertise in this dark website with us. It helps to provide more precise information about Cyber-Guerrilla to our subscribers.

hackerrljqhmq6jb -- Hack Group

If You're facing any difficulty associated with hacking like your pc has been Hacked, or your social websites account was hacked and cheated in online date site. And searching for skilled assistance, then it is possible to think about this dark link. Even they supply some distinctive hacking training too. They charge for each and every service. It is possible to assess their support cost at the pricing department. And should you want any exceptional service, you may contact them with a given email at the service page. Main services that they offer are hacking, social networking risks, computer surveillance and hacking, eliminate a connection, find missing people, background checks, SSN trace, Internet dating scams, Cyberbully --cyberstalked, computer security training, cyber extortion, associations, monitoring, passwords and Cyber fraud.

Note: Before purchasing their solutions, read testimonials about them discuss their services at almost any hacking dark forum.

hackcanl2o4lvmnv -- Hack Canada

Hack Canada is just another go-to destination in the

concealed web to find out hacking. Here is a lot of hacking information accessible. If you're really eager to find out hacking, then pay a visit to this dark link. They have a lot of hacking tutorials and files. Their database is actually huge in itself.

vb75uj2ap3hyyava -- Hacking is Art

Want to find out a few progress tech tips and tricks then need to stop by this Dark website connection. You can check all covered subjects by click on articles. They do not post much anything they post has a great deal of information and superior stull also. Lately cover subjects with this dark site are Safe USB boot using Debian, Ethereum GPU Mining on Linux, Amazon MP3 Downloader, and 64-bit Linux, Battlefield 2 with Job Truth About Windows 7 and a lot more. If these subjects interest you, then you may go to this concealed onion link to find out more at the same subjects in profound.

fsv2bgli7wk4hkvl -- Team Hacking

If You're Looking for some finest dark net links that having escaped, dumps and hacking information, you need to contemplate Team Hacking onion connection. See once to learn more about this profound link.

blackhost5xlrhev -- BlackHost

This dark site is developed through an Italian developer. BlackHost provides You some wonderful services sharing documents, send email anonymously, BF & Ook! Interpreter, Ciphers, Converters, Crypters, Hashes, and Password Strenght Meter etc.. If you're interested in scripts to perform a specific job, then you have to stop by this site. Since they've vase set of scripts. This dark site is well user friendly and organized. If you like to play with the game, you'll love this. Here I discovered a fantastic game, they also call it Hacker Game. I am sure that you will adore this particular onion connection to many things.

4xzg7em4btak4lnu -- Hackers Collective

This dark site has some best hackers. If You're Looking for Best deep internet links to employ a hacker for any hacking job, you can think about Hackers Collective. They've split their hackers into 3 classes Grade C hackers, Grade B Hackers, Grade A Hackers. Services charges are based on Group under that you hacking job come. Most supplied services by these are hacking of Facebook, Twitter and other social networking reports, hacking of email accounts, DOS attacks of unprotected sites, hacking University databases, control and hack private in addition to corporate computers and a lot more. To find out more about their solutions, take a look at this onion link yourself.

yukoni2bjn5woljfeng -- Yukon

If You're Looking for best sources for hacking associated services or employ A hacker on heavy internet, then it is possible to think about this dark link. They're offering several services such as telephone flooding, developing a virus, site hacking, email, Hacking VK, Blind SQLi KUPIVIP.RU, producing viruses and a lot more. This dark site supports multiple languages. Proceed to the speech section and choose which one you know more. For more detail, check this out dark net links yourself.

edfbn5gfuaj2bc2w -- Crypter

Crypter, as the title suggests, it's about to encrypt and decrypt. If You Would like to Send a message in re-type to somebody, then it's possible to take advantage of this dark web website. They assert the algorithm employed in the script is exceptionally developed by their particular group. However, to utilize this support, you will need to enable javascript from Tor Browser.

6f6ejaiiixypfqaf -- Debian Backport

This dark site shares information about Debian. If You Wish to keep upgrade about Debian package, Debian forthcoming news, then bookmark this profound link.

mvfjfugdwgc5uwho -- 0day. Now

This dark site Is an excellent source for vulnerability investigators and safety Professionals because they have an enormous assortment of exploits and vulnerabilities database. If these issues interest you, then this shadowy website is the best source for you.

o4eahdlslz2y6j2q -- Israeli Cyber Army

If You're looking for the best deep link for the hacktivism set, then you can contemplate the above dark web site. This is Called the Israeli Cyber Army. This chief group objective is protecting Israel, country websites, Jewish taxpayers and much more. Their fighting is from them who despise Israel and attempt to damage Israel. The main members of the team are Zurael_STz, Pinkihacks (Official), 4Get. ME, th3ILf4lc0n. If you would like to join these hackers, then it's possible to stop by this dark link to receive their social networking profile hyperlinks.

wqekut2pocn45hwp -- Brotherhood Hackers

This dark net forum link is devoted to hacking. Yes, for your entire hacking Needs, you may stop by this profound forum. You can talk here along with other members of hacking programs, hacking novels, DOXING, and a lot more. In accordance with their existing data, now this dark net forum 387 total articles, 207 complete themes and 1286 absolute members. To learn more, check yourself out.

qkjscem7kksghlux -- Hoe Chi Meow

This dark website accepts information loopholes, diplomatic hacks, Anonymous information Leaks and governmental limited substance etc.. Whether this kind of content attention, then you see given Tor URL to learn more information about this profound link.

ranionjgot5cud3p -- Ranion

Ranion is your next choice from the listing of dim links for hacking. Should you wish to purchase FUD ransomware, then this murky link will be able to assist you. When you buy from them, you receive a completely free Anonymous C&C Dashboard through Onion to handle your customers and additional FREE Customizations. They have four bundles. You are able to purchase anybody in accordance with your requirement. To learn more about their fortunes, you have to see the given Tor URL yourself. They've depth information about every pile at their site.

3fym7qpu7jsljat7 -- Hacking -- HackerLabs: When I assessed these dark links, then unable to observe any helpful details on-site page.

Hc3sz3i2rb5dljqq -- Service/Phone Calling -- Ghost Phone: This profound web site links offer you excellent service that's anonymous phoning if you would like to secrete phoning to one to a single individual with no guys in center tracking this website can supply you ghost calling support. To learn more, you may go to this fantastic deep web sites.

Mre36vzwos4nng3h -- Tools Automobile Hacker

If You're Looking for a deep link that offers automobile hacking tools, then you Can consider this site. Tools that which they provide are Reverse IP, Drupal Mass Exploiter, Revslider Mass Exploiter, Zone-h Mass Notifier, Defacer ID Mass Notifier, Wp-Brute Force, Shell Scanner, CSRF Exploiter, Bing Dorking, Com_User Scanner and a Lot More. Before using any instrument, please read testimonials about them in darknet or you could combine any forum and talk with other members of the automobile hacking tools. Therefore, if you're likely to utilize any given instrument, do at your own risk.

Bylu6d6nx3og7shy -- Safety without Borders

Safety without Borders's Most Important aim is to help individuals and businesses That are battling against human rights abuse, racism, ethnicity, and sexuality etc.. They do not bill any single penny for their solutions.

If you want their help, you can use the Request Assistance button and the following form. In case you have any hacking abilities too and wish to utilize your abilities for good. You could also combine this dark site. To learn more, visit the given onion connection yourself after.

CHAPTER FIVE
THREAT INTELLIGENCE

The dark net (also called the darknet) is often associated with pictures of Midnight hackers and nervous villains working in isolation. In fact, the deep net and darknet are hives of bronchial activity spanning all hours. All these regions of the net are used by men and women looking for anonymity for many different reasons, both illegal and legal in character.

Safety professionals and public security officials have a vested interest in Discovering threat intellect on the deep internet and darknet. This intelligence enables organizations to discover and avoid threats of all types --But, just what would be the deep net and dim net?

Which Are Your Deep Web And Darknet And How Can They Function?

The deep net , occasionally called the invisible web, comprises Sites and information sources which are unindexed and non-discoverable by internet search engines, like Google, within the outside net. The deep web is anticipated to be 400-500 times the magnitude of the surface net.

The deep net includes online pages which are limited by

passwords and Paywalls (for instance, private social networking accounts and internet banking dashboards), or encrypted and dynamic networks. The expression"deep net" isn't interchangeable with all the darknet/dark net --it comprises that the darknet/dark web.

The darknet/dark net is a hidden subsection of this Deep net. It requires special applications, including a Tor browser, to get. The dark screen offers users complete anonymity. That is the reason a fantastic deal of intense activity, such as illegal merchandise sales, human manipulation, and conversation around prohibited subjects, happens there.

Obtaining the darknet Isn't illegal in itself, Though dark net Actions are usually prohibited. User anonymity means the darknet can be occasionally employed for less harmful activities, like preventing government censorship and protecting whistleblowers.

Contrary to popular belief, darknet information Isn't Hard to get --but it Is rather tricky to navigate because pages aren't indexed or controlled. Inexpert darknet browsing could be harmful, and finding anything useful or specific is very time-consuming.

How Can The Darknet Achieve User Anonymity?

Darknet users attain anonymity using onion routing. An individual's information is routed Through multiple layers of encryption before reaching its destination, making its source anonymous. These encryption layers are somewhat similar to the layers of an onion.

Tor (an acronym for"The Onion Router"), the hottest dark browser, Uses this encryption procedure. Tor is a free program browser that hides the consumer's IP address, which simplifies any private or metadata collection.

What Do Deep Web And Darknet Websites Look Like?

Most Websites and printed information on the deep internet and darknet take the form of a market, discussion forum, or even broken data dump:

Marketplaces make it possible for consumers to anonymously buy and sell prohibited products on the darknet.

Chat forums make it possible for consumers to anonymously discuss prohibited subjects, like the way to run cyber attacks, or how to manufacture illegal substances.

Breached info loopholes, such as broken private or business information, are shared on deep internet sites like Pastebin.

What Can Information Sources Be Found The Deep Web And Darknet?

You will find several information networks that can be found on the deep web and darknet. Below you'll get a listing of data suppliers, including popular sites and websites within them. This listing isn't exhaustive--websites are constantly changing as they're added or removed.

Deep Web Networks

OpenBazaar Is a decentralized, open market marketplace established in 2016. The system's objective is to prevent the"middleman" involved with surface internet trade. Buyers and sellers on OpenBazaar utilize cryptocurrencies and participate straight to avoid fees related to typical payment methods such as Paypal. You will find over 20,000 vendors on OpenBazaar with consumer action across 150 nations.

OpenBazaar Isn't inherently anonymizing but may be

retrieved via Tor if users want anonymity. The system doesn't appeal to illegal exchanges, and the majority of its trades aren't prohibited. But as it's decentralized, OpenBazaar has no method to correctly track or cope with unlawful action. Illegal OpenBazaar listings aren't indexed and aren't always reachable by search engines inside the market.

Telegram is a cloud-based Immediate messaging, Voice, and video messaging support very similar to WhatsApp. It is regarded as among the very secure messaging programs for many reasons:

Chats may be ruined while the dialog ends, or be deleted using a self-destruct timer.

Telegram boasts three layers of encryption, rather than the normal two layers complemented by other messaging programs.

Telegram Provides access to their own API, which opens up infinite possibilities for People to make games, get alarms, produce data visualizations, construct Customized tools, and even exchange obligations between consumers. API entry to Telegram Means that several of the discussions in public classes are mainly Discoverable to associations collecting open-source intelligence out of internet sources.

With over 200 million active users, it's not surprising that Telegram is a favorite place to hold talks about illegal activities. There have been a lot of reports of phishing scammers utilizing Telegram because of their way of touch with sufferers.

Discord is a voiceover IP and messaging App with 200 million active users. Discord's user interface resembles a cross between Skype and Slack. It is totally free to use and can be obtained as a net, mobile, and desktop program. Inside Discord, users may produce their own servers and server personal, password-protected, or public stations inside these servers.

Discord Has been criticized for being exposed to strikes from cybercriminals. Beyond safety problems, the discussions happening on Discord have evolved to include mature, narcotic, or NSFW (Not Safe For Work) content. Discord is connected to talks about illegal activity in addition to the alt-right motion. Back in August 2017, it had been found as a preparation tool for coordinating the"Unite the Right" rally in Charlottesville, VA..

The IRC (Web Relay Chat) is an instant messaging program developed for large numbers of customers to communicate in real-time. It was made in 1988 and has diminished in popularity since 2003 as more consumers move to social networking platforms along with other messaging tools. The IRC still has close to 500 million active users and 250,000 stations. The IRC has been associated with illegal file trading, denial of service (DoS) attacks and trojan/virus infections.

The IRC Is not inherently designed for anonymity. Users should use a virtual private network (VPN) or get into the IRC via Tor to attain consumer anonymity.

The Open Internet can be described within an open network that's decentralized (management is shared by several parties), reachable (anybody can participate without asking permission), and open (anybody can modify or enhance it).

It may also be characterized by what it is not: the net's"walled gardens" where the material is controlled and monetized (Facebook and Google, by way of instance). These walled gardens offer a simpler and much more curated consumer experience. Still, in the price of particular liberty --algorithms control what material is printed, and publishers are limited to solutions that are constructed from the websites.

Content On the open internet is publicly available but not always indexed by standard search engines such as Google. These are website examples on the Open Internet with webpages which might not be found:

4chan: an imageboard website with themes that range from video games. 4chan is also connected with subcultures and activism classes, like the alt-right and denial of service (DoS) cyber strikes.

Craigslist: a classifieds website utilized for hosting discussion forums and promotion products, services, housing, and employment. Scams and earnings of stolen or counterfeit products aren't rare on Craigslist.

Leolist: a classifieds website often used by sex workers. It's been associated with human trafficking cases.

Pastebin: famous for hosting torrents, hacking information dumps and hyperlinks to darknet websites.

Dark Internet Networks

Tor was created by the U.S. Naval Research Laboratory in

the 1990's planning to empower stable government communications. It is now the most widely used system for surfing the dark net. Tor websites have .onion as their top-notch domain name. These are well known .onion websites:

Tor Discussion Forums

8chan was established in 2013 and gained traction following 4chan banned articles related to Gamergate (a prevalent harassment campaign against girls and progressivism from the gambling community). 8chan functions as an internet hate-group for nationalists, neo-nazis, alt-righters, and misogynists to maintain anonymous talks. Read: What's 8chan and Why Should You Care?

The Website Is also connected with the 2019 Christchurch mosque along with San Diego synagogue shootings. The latter's perpetrator posted links to his manifesto and Facebook webpage before committing the assault. The website contains 35,000 daily customers.

The Daily Stormer is much like 8chan: it is an anonymous comment forum for white-supremacists, anti-semites, and neo-nazis. It was founded in July 2013 and proceeded into the darknet in August 2017. The website is well known for online trolling and coordinating harassment campaigns. It had been used to help arrange the"Unite the Right" rally in Charlottesville, Virginia in 2017.

Dread resembles the darknet's Reddit. It's modeled closely following Reddit, including sub-communities and consumer moderators. The website is a forum, not a market --but contains talks on generating prohibited chemicals, recommended traders, and which other Tor websites are run by scammers or have been forged.

Tor Marketplaces

Hydra is a Russian-language Darknet market with individual vendor stores. The website takes steps to prevent people and law enforcement from entering; it calms Russian sellers that are eager to cover hosting fees, also promotes trusted vendor-buyer communication before trades occur.

Nightmare Marketplace was established in 2018 and contained listings for drugs, stolen info, counterfeit products, and many different other prohibited trades. The Marketplace affirms escrow (third-party trade arrangements) and includes an affiliated conversation forum.

Silk Road 3.1 is a widely-used substitute for the original

Silk Road, which was closed down in 2013. Of 50,000 listings, more than half are linked to prohibited substances.

I2P (Invisible Internet Project) is an anonymizing system that concentrates on protected internal connections and consumer communicating instead of monitoring goods. Its principal function is to become a"network over the net" with visitors comprised within its boundaries. From the I2P network, hosted sites are called "eepsites" and also have .i2p as their top-notch domain name.

ZeroNet is a peer-to-peer system started in 2015. Every network peer acts as a host, which makes it decentralized and resistant to censorship. ZeroNet isn't inherently anonymous-- users may attain anonymity via Tor. It is also accessible; any user may clone and make their own variants of websites within ZeroNet.

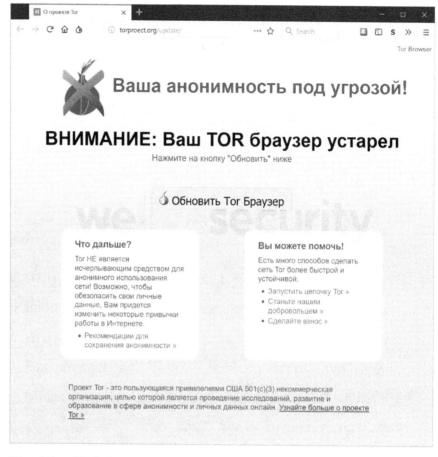

ZeroNet Websites are based on the next ZeroNet sample websites :

ZeroBlog: for editing and creating decentralized sites

ZeroTalk: for generating decentralized forums

ZeroMail: for participating in encoded peer-reviewed communication

ZeroMe: for decentralized microblogging, very similar to Twitter

ReactionGIFs: for peer-reviewed document sharing

ZeroChat: for participating in real-time two-way conversation messaging

Zeropolls: enables users to generate, vote and see surveys

ZeroWiki: a ZeroNet-focused wiki where users may create and edit themes

What Threats Are Current On The Web And Darknet?

What Exactly are offenders doing about the dark net? Most corporate security specialists and public security officials are trying to find offenses and evidence of crimes associated with stolen and stolen products, conducting human and drug trafficking, planning strikes, promoting and draining data and data, money laundering, and fraud.

The Following are a few specific examples of darknet action:

Discussing and selling"How-To" guides. Guides can pay for everything from how to create an illegal material, to the way to run fraud from a company.

Releasing or promoting personal information. Personal information breaches are generally utilized to obtain access to bank accounts or may be used to target people for harassment (called"doxxing").

Purchasing and selling fraudulent tax records. Cybercriminals will frequently buy and submit false tax records before the actual taxpayer is ready to.

Exposing national safety information, such as protection strategies, weapon programs or construction patterns related to federal security.

Leaking or stealing source code. This makes it much easier for hackers to find out whether there are some vulnerabilities in your associations' working systems or safety programs.

Selling"Publish" templates. Spoofing templates make it possible for visitors to create fake sites or types on behalf of a company as a way to collect private information.

Exposing business databases. This escapes sensitive details regarding employee balances, in addition to an organization's overall footprint, such as partnerships and personal contracts.

Implementing for prohibited actions, for example hitman providers or human trafficking.

Purchasing and selling illegal products or materials.

Seeing and measuring child porn.

CHAPTER SIX
WHAT'S TOR AND THE DEEP WEB?

A Really Basic Description of this Online

The World Wide Web, in its simplest form, is a set of computers talking to each other. Computer A asks Pc B to get a piece of data, and Pc B sends it back. This bit of advice might be a page, an ad, a calculation--nearly anything.

Every computer employs an exceptional name in this communication. That title is an IP address (IP stands for Internet Protocol, it's formatted like this: 29.75.148.222). IP addresses are not very memorable, therefore that they appear in the kind of an internet address. By way of instance, when you sort "facebook.com," your own Internet Service Provider requires that petition (from Computer A) and translates that domain to the IP address corresponding to your Facebook server (Computer B). Facebook (Computer B) subsequently gives Computer A the data that is searched.

This communication method is used Throughout the World Wide Web, including the profound Net and dark net. The gap between the deep net and the remainder of the world wide web is whether you can hunt for it.

The Deep Web Requires The Surface Internet

Internet users may use Google to search for Facebook, CapitalOne, or even TSN. The results of those searches are cases of pages that are indexed. Anything which may be found using standard search engines has been considered surface webpages.

Users can not, however, Look for a dialog their adolescent had on WhatsApp a week, nor will they hunt to find the contents of a personal email or banking site, or perhaps some classifieds websites. Another illustration of unsearchable information is that the idiotic chatter that computers always churns outside to check on the status, health, or functionality of different computers, or other gear in a method.

This information comprises nearly all the deep net. It is mostly boring Information that's not helpful for the vast majority of individuals. According to some sources, the searchable surface net only constitutes about 10 percent of the Web --that the deep net includes the remaining 90 percent.

The Deep Internet vs. The Dark Internet

The phrases"deep net" and"dark web" (sometimes called the darknet) Are frequently used interchangeably, however they're incredibly different. The dark net forms a small portion of the deep internet, as exemplified by the infamous iceberg metaphor. Like the deep net, it includes unsearchable webpages --but was created intentionally to make consumer anonymity, and requires special tools to get. User anonymity enables illegal actions to flourish, and that's the way the dark net gets its poor reputation.

All these"dark" regions of the heavy web began well before the Web was Mainstream and popular. Early Internet users wrapped out in online chatrooms known as Internet Relay Chats (IRC). Some criminal action on the dark net today arose from those IRC communities.

The darknet is not exclusively used for promoting drugs and using open Talks about neo-nazism; nevertheless --it may be used by anybody seeking anonymity. This may comprise whistleblowers protecting their individuality when discharging information, or consumers looking the net freely in a state where certain content may be censored or obstructed.

Provided that a user understands where they are going (ie. they have a connection), they could Readily get an unindexed deep webpage. But even if a user may discover a link into a dark website, they can not get that page at a traditional browser like Chrome or even Firefox.

It is worth mentioning that, while the iceberg metaphor helps distinguish Surface, heavy, and dark net sites, it is not a true depiction of how they function. In fact, all of them operate alongside each other as opposed to in compartmentalized segments of electronic space. To put it differently, black and deep sites are concealed, or procured, in plain view--security through obscurity.

Getting the Dark Internet: Tor

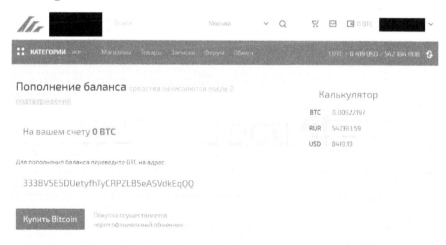

The SilkRoad Was an infamous dark net marketplace that has been closed down with an FBI sting in November of 2014. What made SilkRoad a dark site?

To get into dark Sites, users should use Tor. Tor is an online browser, which appears much like any other online browser, but provides users anonymity. It does this via a procedure called onion routing (the acronym"Tor" stands for"the skillet").

Tor compels a pc to conduct its communications via a High Number of Other computers, called nodes, even until they're led into the last computer. Nodes, also known as relays, maybe any computer that's been installed using Tor applications (you can actually download it here).

Traveling through numerous nodes means that from the time a communicating gets To its destination, it's not possible to ascertain its first place or IP address. This provides users complete anonymity while surfing. The numerous nodes routing communications signify multiple layers of"the onion" in Tor.

Onion routing also usually means that the browser works very slowly. Users can See any website URL (even surface sites) from the Tor browser, but dim website links (that have .onion as their top-notch domain name, instead of. Com) should be seen in Tor.

Who constructed Tor? Can it be a key set of hackers?

Actually, it had been the US Government. The US Government developed and elegant Tor browser technologies to protect their own anonymity and communicating stations:

"The core principle supporting Tor, specifically,' onion routing,' was initially Financed by the US Office of Naval Research in 1995, and also the maturation of the technology was assisted by DARPA in 1997." --Joseph Babatunde Fagoyinbo.

Tor was eventually Released into the general public in 2002.

Could Tor Be Hacked? Is There a Way to "Break" the Anonymity?

Yes and no. It's not possible to hack on the Tor algorithm, so far as we understand. It may be monitored backward through the maze of computers into the origin --but this awkward process would take decades to finish.

People are fallible, so it Is Far Easier to"hack" Tor's Human operators compared to hack the machine. By way of instance, SilkRoad needed a nearly ideal system. If it were not for a series of lucky hints, and errors made by the creator, it'd probably still be operating.

For a similarly intriguing story, WW2s Enigma machine was just cracked from an investigation of human character.

Tor also does not shield Users from downloading malware which broadcasts unique places to prospective attackers. This means there's potential for consumer identity, particularly amateur user identities, to be subjected to the dark net.

It's also likely to Discover if someone is using Tor (this Isn't accurate for Very sophisticated adversaries) by monitoring exit nodes. An exit node is a final computer that an individual strikes before seeing a target website. Most Tor exit nodes are well understood and mapped with rational certainty. For a similarly intriguing story, WW2s Enigma system was just cracked from an investigation of human character.

Tor does not shield users from possibly downloading malware that Broadcasts unique places to prospective attackers.

You can also find out if someone is using Tor (this Isn't true for very Sophisticated adversaries), nevertheless, by monitoring exit nodes. An exit node is a final computer that an individual strikes before visiting a target website. Most Tor exit nodes are well understood and mapped. Consequently, exit nodes could be mapped with reasonable certainty.

What's Information about the Deep Web and Dark Internet Useful?

Given that the consumer anonymity and lack of searchability on the deep internet and dim Net, it is not surprising that these sites offer invaluable data sources for detecting bad actors in many different crimes. This can be hugely helpful for an assortment of businesses, from law enforcement to retail chains.

By Way of Example, the deep internet hosts talk forums inciting hate address, Used to target people, arrange physical dangers, host precursory files, or discuss illegal activities, including shoplifting and drug use/sales. Glue websites, for example, Pastebin, which aren't indexed, are a fantastic spot to find signs of information breaches. There is also a number of unindexed pages on sites, which frequently contain adult services connected to human trafficking or stolen products for sale.

The dark net takes prohibited actions even further: although Lots of dark web Websites are now scams, also, there are marketplaces selling medications, breached information, child porn, and several other illegal products and services. The dark net also includes quite a few forums and news/commentary websites where users publicly exchange dangerous suggestions and possible threats.

Since the deep internet is unindexed, and also the dark net is awkward and Dangerous to browse, public security officials should use technical tools, for example, Beacon, to get relevant content securely and economically.

To Sum Up:

The World Wide Web is relatively easy.

The deep internet is HUGE. It's also fairly dull.

The dark net is a little section of the deep web that's created for anonymity and thus harbors illegal action.

Dark things do occur on the deep internet, but not quite as far as the press wants us to believe.

Data on the deep internet and shadowy net are tremendously valuable for associations (for example, law enforcement) searching for possible dangers, from data breaches to drug trafficking.

Would you like to effectively search through articles on the deep internet and dim Net, and accomplish this safely? Beacon permits you to extract crucial information from the darkened net in just a couple of clicks. Reserve a demonstration to find out more.

CHAPTER SEVEN
DARK WEB SEARCH FOR YOUR OSINT STRATEGY

Are You Tracking For Information Leaks About The Dark Internet?

When it's your job to protect people and resources, the Dark Internet (or even Darknet) is a significant area to browse. Dark net Information is an essential component for safety and threat intelligence, along with the staff at Echosec have assembled a tool to look for it. Beacon is your OSINT tool that delivers structured dark net data. With Beacon, you're able to quickly sift through the rubble and surface the data that matters to your company.

The Issue With Dark Internet Data

Darknet information Isn't Hard to get , but It's very hard to search. Since the dark net is non- indexed, the material inside it's disorganized, which makes it hard to expose anything special. Searching the dark net with no ideal OSINT instrument is time-consuming to say the least.

The Option - A Dark Search Engine

Beacon is a totally indexed dark net tool that ingests heaps of resources including sites, code repositories, and databases. Constructed from the engineers in Echosec, a pioneer in data discovery, Beacon is your newest way to locate crucial intelligence on the shadowy net.

Contrary to Echosec, Beacon hunts for files, instead of real-time information. This historical perspective provides users a comprehensive eye-line to the hidden knowledge of the dark net. This makes Beacon a valuable companion to the Echosec platform.

Beacon is unique since it uses natural language processing (NLP) to Dark web statistics. NLP enables the instrument to extract things from the material. Entities include matters like individuals, locations, organizations, telephone numbers, and social security numbers.

Through extracting and indexing information, Beacon constructs an inner Knowledge chart. This permits you to adhere to a thing across distinct domains, social networking, and other sites across the internet.

What Can You Do With This Info?

With organized dark net data, users may make inferences about a thing and Its use throughout the net. As an instance, it is possible to locate an email address and follow the use of the email address around networks.

This capability is particularly beneficial for a use case such as brand protection. Analysts can conduct a search for their news on the dark net and expose any harmful details. Stolen email addresses, violated NDAs, categorized info, and counterfeit products are simply the tip of this iceberg.

Executive security professionals may search for leaked info related to their clientele. The information they find can vary from hacked email, leaked passwords, or login info from societal profiles.

WHY Dark Internet Data Topics

Reduction avoidance for Retailers: Beacon will reveal to you where your products have been sold illegally and who's selling them.

Corporate Safety : Locate NDA offenses and other private information that's been revealed on the darknet.

Insurance: Data leaks are a significant legal liability. Tracking open info in the darknet lets you proactively take PR steps if leaks occur.

Finance & Fraud: Leaked credit cards, IDs, reused passwords, and balances. Give offenders an attack vector to monetary accounts. Beacon permits you to find threats to your organization and risks to your clients. Getting conscious of any dangers lets you better protect your company and customers.

General criminal action: The darknet is home to a profusion of prohibited products purchased and sold on the internet. Beacon provides insight into what's being dispersed in communities anywhere.

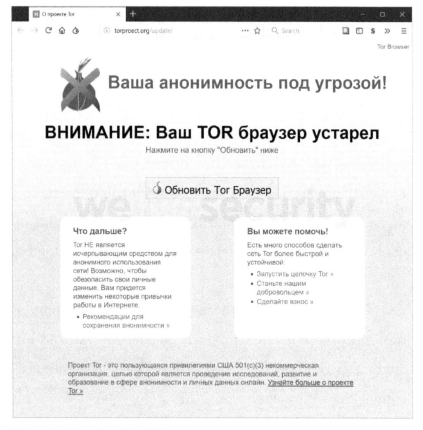

Illuminating the Dark Internet

Beacon provides contextualized data in the sea of data that is disgusting. This OSINT instrument for your darknet lets you quickly find the information that matters to you.

Using a trojanized version of a formal Tor Browser bundle, the Cybercriminals supporting this effort have been quite successful -- thus much their pastebin.com accounts have experienced over 500,000 viewpoints and they could steal

US$40,000+ in bitcoins.

Malicious domains

This recently detected trojanized Tor Browser was dispersing using two Sites that claimed they disperse the official Russian language edition of this Tor Browser. The very first such site displays a message from Russian asserting the visitor has an obsolete Tor Browser. The information is shown if the visitor gets the most up-to-date Tor Browser variant.

Translated Into English:

Your Anonymity is at risk! WARNING: Your Tor Browser is obsolete Click on the button"Update"

On Clicking the"Update Tor Browser" button, the visitor will be redirected into another site with the potential for downloading a Windows installer. There are not any signs that the exact same site has spread Linux, macOS or cellular variations.

These two domain names -- tor-browser[.] org and torproect[.] Org -- were made in 2014. The malicious domain torproect[.] Org domain name is quite much like the true torproject.org; it is only missing one letter. For Russian-speaking sufferers, the message may raise no distress on account of the simple fact that"torprotect" resembles a transliteration from the Cyrillic. But, it doesn't seem like criminals relied upon typosquatting, since they encouraged these 2 sites on several resources.

Distribution

Back in 2017 and ancient 2018 cybercriminals encouraged the pages of this Trojanized Tor Browser using junk messages on several different Russian forums. These messages include various themes, such as darknet markets, cryptocurrencies, net privacy and censorship jump. Especially, a few of the notes mention Roskomnadzor, a Russian government thing for censorship in telecommunications and media.

In April And March 2018, the offenders began to utilize the pastebin.com web support to market the two domains linked to the imitation Tor Browser page. Mainly, they made four reports and created plenty of pastes optimized for search engines to rank them high for phrases that cover subjects like medications, cryptocurrency, censorship skip, as well as the titles of Russian politicians.

The thought behind this is that a possible victim would carry out an internet search for particular keywords and, at some stage, see a paste that is created. Each such glue has a header which boosts the bogus site.

This translates into English:

BRO, download Tor Browser so the Cops will not watch you. Regular browsers reveal what you're viewing, even through proxies and VPN plug-ins. Tor encrypts all visitors and moves it via arbitrary servers from all over the world. It's more dependable than VPN or proxy and simplifies most of the Roskomnadzor censorship. This is official Tor Browser site: torproect[.] Org Tor Browser using anti-captcha: tor-browser[.] Org Save link

The offenders claim This variant of the Tor Browser has anti-captcha Capacity, but actually this isn't correct.

Each the pastes in the four Unique accounts was seen more than 500,000 times. But it is not feasible for us to state precisely how many viewers actually visited the sites and downloaded from the trojanized version of this Tor Browser.

Diagnosis

This trojanized Tor Browser is a fully functional program. Actually, it Relies on Tor Browser 7.5, which premiered in January 2018. Thus, non-technically-savvy individuals likely won't detect any difference between the first version and also the trojanized one.

No alterations have been made to source code of their Tor Browser; all of Windows binaries Are precisely the same as in the first edition. Nonetheless, these offenders altered the default browser preferences and a few of the extensions.

The offenders want to stop victims from upgrading the trojanized Tor Version into a more recent version, as in this instance it'll be upgraded to some non-trojanized, legitimate variant. That is the reason why they disabled all sorts of upgrades in the configurations, and also renamed the updater tool out of updater.exe into updater.exe0.

Besides the altered update configurations, the offenders shifted the Default User-Agent into the distinctive hardcoded value:

Mozilla/5.0 (Windows NT 6.1; rv:77777.0) Gecko/20100101

Firefox/52.0

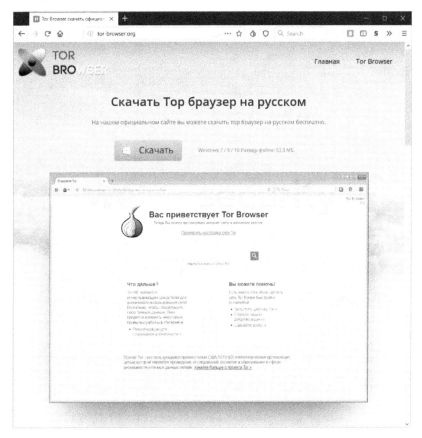

All of trojanized Tor Browser sufferers will utilize the Identical User-Agent; hence it may Be applied as a fingerprint from the offenders to discover, on the server-side, if the sufferer is utilizing this trojanized version.

The most essential change is to this xpinstall.signatures. Required Configurations, which disable an electronic signature check for set up Tor Browser add-ons. Hence, the attackers may alter any add-on and it'll be loaded with the browser with no complaint about it neglecting its electronic signature test.

```
pref("app.update.auto",false);
pref("app.update.url","");
pref("app.update.url.details","");
pref("app.update.url.manual","");
pref("app.update.url...",...,...);
pref("extensions.update.background.url",false);
pref("extensions.update.enabled",false);
pref("...sync.prefs.sync.extensions.update.enabled",false);
pref("extensions.update.background.url","");
pref("extensions.update.url","");
pref("media.gmp-manager.url","");
pref("app.update.enabled",false);
pref("xpinstall.signatures.required",false);
pref("xpinstall.whitelist.required",false);
pref("...sync.prefs.sync.xpinstall.signatures.required",false);
pref("webextensions.storage.sync.serverURL","");
pref("extensions.blocklist.enabled",false);
pref("extensions.blocklist.itemURL","");
pref("extensions.blocklist.url","");
pref("app.update.url.details","");
//pref("browser.startup.homepage","http://onionbxthphlyzyp.onion/start");
//pref("browser.startup.homepage","about:tor");
pref("general.useragent.override","Mozilla/5.0 (Windows NT 6.1; rv:77777.0) Gecko/20100101 Firefox/52.0");
```

Moreover, the offenders altered the HTTPS Everywhere add-on comprised With the browser, especially its manifest.json file. The modification provides a material script (script.js) which will be implemented on load at the context of each page.

This injected script informs a C&C server concerning the present webpage downloads and addresses a JavaScript payload which will be implemented in the context of this current page. The C&C host is on an onion domain name, so it is available only through Tor.

As the offenders behind this effort understand what site the sufferer is Currently seeing, they could function distinct JavaScript payloads for various sites. But, that isn't the situation here during our study, the JavaScript payload was consistently precisely the exact same for many pages we have seen.

The JavaScript payload functions as a Normal web inject, Meaning That it can interact with all the Website content and execute certain actions. As an instance, it may do a form catching, scrape, conceal or inject the content of a page that is visited, display bogus messages, etc..

But It Ought to Be noted that the de-anonymization of a sufferer is a difficult task since the JavaScript payload is operating in the context of their Tor Browser and doesn't have access to this actual IP address or other bodily qualities of the victim system.

Darknet markets

The sole JavaScript payload We've seen goals three of the biggest Russian-speaking darknet markets. This payload tries to change QIWI (a favorite Russian currency transfer service) or even bitcoin wallets found on webpages of those markets.

Deep net, Dark net and DarkNet

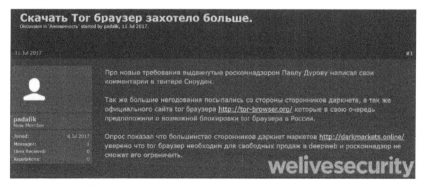

Internet is quite huge and also what we use on daily basis is merely a chunk of it. The worldwideweb is a lot more than this but, an individual ought to be apparent with the gap between the Web and the internet.

Online is your set of various smaller networks Where each node is a host, notebook, smartphone etc..

Internet: In previous days of Web, data was utilized to transport across The worldwideweb, but no Internet existed at the point but in 1989, Tim Berners-Lee introduced the Internet that may be employed to get hyperlinked text or webpages. So, essentially Web is a program that runs over the net to supply this support.

But Web does not include just the site like Facebook, Google, Geeksforgeeks etc.. All these are at the surface net that may be found by search engines. It merely constitutes 4-6percent of the entire web. Section of the WWW that isn't indexed by a search engine such as Google is Deep Internet and it around 500-600 times bigger than the surface net. This internet may only be obtained with a particular link and also with special permission such as information within our cloud driveway can't be found on Google, an individual can't hunt for it. There's a subset of this net named Dark Internet.

Deep Internet: It's the net that can't be obtained by the internet search engines, such as government personal information, financial data, cloud information etc.. These data are private and sensitive, therefore stored out of reach. It's used to offer access to some specific to a particular group of individuals.

```
text  8.88 KB

 1.  # скачать тор браузер windows #
 2.  ┳ ᒯ ᒯ ‐ ᒥ ᒯ ᒯ ‖ ᒹ ᒥ ᒯ
 3.  ‖ ‖ ‖ ‐ ┠ ‖ � � ┠ ‖
 4.  ‖ � ᑯ ‐ ᑯ ᑯ ‖ ᒧ ᒧ ┗ ᑯ
 5.
 6.  ## БРО, качай тор браузер чтобы менты тебя не пасли. ##
 7.  Обычные браузеры видно что ты смотришь, даже через прокси и впн плагины.
 8.  Тор шифрует весь трафик и пропускает его через случайные сервера со всего мира.
 9.  Это надежней чем впн или прокси и обходит все блокировки роскомнадзора.
10.
11.  ## Вот официальный сайт Тор Браузер ##
12.
13.  http://torproect.org
14.
15.  ## Тор браузер с антикапчей ##
16.
17.  http://tor-browser.org
18.
19.
20.  Сохрани ссылку.
```

Dark Web: It's a network construct over the net which is encrypted. Darknet provides anonymity to consumers. 1 these darknet is Tor (The Onion Router). The unique software is needed to enter this system, such as the Tor Browser, which is required to enter the Tor's network. TOR can get regular site too, a site with this network has .onion address. Most hidden services are supplied on Black Web. Friend-to-Friend is just another sort of darknet where two-person transfer information between them. Just concerned individuals have access to it and it's encrypted and password protected. Freenet can also be a darknet that is used for document transport, there are lots of different darknets out there.

Dark Internet: Darknet supply an individual with anonymity; however, service has been Introduced, which enabled someone to sponsor a site on the darknet and stay anonymous. This attracted people who do illegal things to sells items without getting captured. 1 example is a site known as the silk road, which was on darknet named TOR, used to market drugs and has been removed by the FBI.

It May seem a bit frightening, but darknet Is Extremely useful also, for that it had been created, to give anonymity just like to government officer, journalist as well as us.

CHAPTER EIGHT
IMPACT OF DARKNET ON CYBERSECURITY

Not to be mistaken with all the deep net, the darkened web/darknet is a set Of thousands of sites that can not be obtained via ordinary means and are not indexed by search engines such as Google or Yahoo.

In Other Words, That the darknet is an overlay of Programs Which Needs specific Tools and applications to obtain access. The history of this darknet predates the 1980s. The expression was initially utilized to refer to computers on ARPANET, which were concealed and programmed to get messages, but that didn't respond to or admit anything, therefore remaining undetectable or even at the dark. Ever since that time,"darknet" has become an umbrella term that refers to the elements of the world wide web intentionally open to public opinion or concealed networks whose structure is superimposed on the world wide web.

Paradoxically, the darknet's development can be tracked marginally into the U.S. Army. The most typical method to get the darknet is via tools like the Tor network. The system routing capabilities the Tor system utilizes were created in the mid-

1990s by both mathematicians and computer scientists in the U.S. Naval Research Laboratory with the objective of shielding U.S. intelligence communications on the internet.

USE AND ACCESS

Programs of this darknet are almost as broad and as varied as the net: Everything from email and also societal media to sharing and hosting documents, news sites and e-commerce. Accessing it requires particular applications, configurations or consent, frequently using nonstandard communicating protocols and interfaces. Presently, two of the most well-known approaches to get the darknet is through two overlay networks. The first is that the above Tor; the next is known as I2P.

Tor that stands for"onion " or"onion routing" was created Mostly to keep users anonymous. The same as the layers of an onion, information is saved within several layers of encryption. Each coating shows another relay until the last film sends the data to its destination. Info is sent bi-directionally, so data has been shipped back and forth through precisely the exact same tunnel. On any given day, more than a million users are busy on the Tor network.

Bitcoin Address Addresses are identifiers which you use to send bitcoins to another person.

Summary		Transactions		
Address	3CEfsumJOdqSEgSLNoPoywWjvliiYqre	No. Transactions	371	
Hash 160	7bh88e5e6Rczb43ac6069c94d7bdje0b8bibe9d0	Total Received	2.65574657 BTC	
		Final Balance	0.00014 BTC	
		Request Payment	Donation Button	

I2P, which stands for the Invisible Internet Project, was created for User-to-user document sharing. It requires information and encapsulates it in multiple layers. The same as a bit of garlic, data is bunched along with other people's data to stop de-packing and review, and it transmits that information using a unidirectional tunnel.

WHAT'S OUT THERE?

As stated before, the darknet Offers news, e-commerce Websites, and Hosting and email solutions. Though lots of the providers are naive and are only alternatives to what could be discovered on the world wide web, a section of the darknet is extremely nefarious and attached to illegal actions because of the surreptitious nature. Because of this, since the 1990s, cybercriminals have found that a"digital home" on the darknet as a means to communicate, organize and, most lately, decorate the artwork of cyberattacks into a vast assortment of non-stop novices.

Among the most Well-known providers are email providers, which have observed a Dramatic increase recently that parallels the greater prevalence of ransomware. Cyberattackers will frequently use these email services to perform their own attempts to stay hidden from governments.

Hosting providers are yet another. Like the cloud computing Environments that businesses might use within the IT infrastructure, darknet hosting providers are leveraged by cybercriminals and hackers to sponsor sites or e-commerce marketplaces that market dispersed denial-of-service (DDoS) applications and solutions. These hosting providers are generally very unstable since they may be"removed" by law enforcement or vigilante hackers to get political, ideological or ethical factors.

Forums also exist to let hackers and criminals possess independent Talks with the intention of understanding exchanging, such as coordinating and organizing DDoS campaigns (like the ones proposed by Anonymous) and/or measuring cyberattack best practices. These forums include a number of technical choices and languages and may be related to specific hazard actors/ classes, hacktivists, attack vectors, etc..

Last, Exactly like the Actual net, darknet search engines, such as Candle as well as Torch, exist to allow consumers to readily find and browse these numerous forums, websites and e-commerce shops.

A DIGITAL STORE

Maybe more than any other agency use, e-commerce Websites on the darknet Have exploded in popularity in recent years on account of the growth of DDoS for service and stresser solutions, leading to enormous profit margins for entrepreneurial hackers. Everything from DDoS attack tools and botnet rentals to"contracting" that the assistance of a hacker is currently available on the darknet.

The outcome? These e-commerce Websites and their goods have commoditized Cyberattacks as well as making them accessible to a vast selection of non-invasive users. Quite often, these solutions have instinctive, GUI-based interfaces that make setting up and launch strikes quick and easy.

Examples abound, however, one instance of DDoS for a service is PutinStresser. PutinStresser Exemplifies the simplicity of accessibility these services have attained and provides prospective buyers with different payment alternatives, detection programs, many different attack vectors and perhaps even chat-based customer care. Botnet rental providers are also accessible -- their expansion paralleling the increase and usage of botnets because 2016. A complete case of a botnet service that's on the darknet is that the Jen X botnet, that was found in 2018.

Costs for all these tools are as varied as the attack vectors that buyers may Buy and vary from as low as $100 to a few thousand dollars. Rates are generally based on several different factors, like the number of attack vectors contained within the ceremony, the dimensions of this assault (Gbps/Tbps) along with the need.

Malware and ransomware are both common. The infamous WannaCry Global ransomware effort had its C2C servers hosted on the darknet. Additionally, like their botnet and DDoS brethren, malware and ransomware possess their very own"pay for play" providers that dramatically simplify the process of starting a ransomware effort. Numerous ransomware providers exist which permit a user to just define the ransom quantity and add letters/notes, and the consumer is provided an easy executable to send to sufferers.

Last, a range of solutions can be obtained, allowing almost anyone with access to the darknet (along with also the capability to convert cash to bitcoin for repayment) to contract hackers to get their job. Services include hacking mails, hacking interpersonal networking reports and designing malicious applications.

A Number of These services revolve around the instruction Vertical. The action of instructional institutions moving their instruction tools and analyzing to internet networks has bred a new generation of students keen to buy the assistance of hackers to alter grades and start DDoS attacks on schools' networks to postpone evaluations.

Can Cloud Protect Against Ransomware?

Ransomware works by assessing a sufferer's documents and holding them hostage Before a bitcoin ransom has been paid. And while cloud is a cheap and effortless option to off-site tape storage, then it isn't adequately protected from ransomware.

Among the biggest benefits of this cloud is really, what if often the biggest concern using a cloud migration: safety. While cloud suppliers are clearly bigger targets, they're also better able to invest from the protection companies that need to guard against aggressive attackers.

To shield against ransomware from the cloud, companies must understand the Shared responsibility model of computing.

Ransomware Can Hit The Cloud

KrebsOnSecurity Given This case research is dependent on the ransomware assault on Children in Film, an advocacy company for kid actors that functioned entirely from application hosting services using a controlled cloud supplier. A worker started an email attachment which seemed to add a statement -- in actuality, it had been the payload.

The Fastest Way To Cloud To Ransomware Protection

The cloud may work for copies; however, rather than just backing up your files into the cloud, use numerous clouds concurrently to enlarge protections and decrease risk -- without radically increasing prices.

A committed cybersecurity and disaster recovery approach is also critical to Employing the cloud and efficiently. By knowing your baseline cybersecurity position, you're better able to recognize gaps and minimize risks. Should you take some opportunity to identify and categorize your software, you'll get a better feeling of RTOs and RPOs, allowing a more targeted emergency recovery approach.

Our team of specialists understands backup and disaster restoration, cybersecurity, and The cloud proceed hand-in-hand. Speak to our specialists in a free one-on-one virtual or on-site whiteboard session to find out what we have to offer you.

Is USENET Part of this Deepnet?

Deepnet, DarkNet, along with other similar provisions, have been in the press a lot recently. Most famously, the cookie group Anonymous shot down several websites on the DarkNet, which were distributing illegal content. It has made several individuals understandably interested in precisely what the Deepnet is. It is not USENET, that is becoming obvious as you begin to comprehend exactly how and why the Deepnet or even DarkNet exist.

Obtaining Indexed

You may Have heard terms such as"search engine optimization", "SEO" and"search engine optimization on your journeys throughout the net. These are fields that are related to accessing search engines to detect them, so, to include those sites to the search engine indexes. It is actually quite a lot of work to have a search engine to detect you; it is challenging to stick out among countless websites! Among the methods that search engines index a website is by following links from other websites that result in it.

On the USENET method, the whole purpose of owning a newsgroup would be to get it inserted to as many servers as you possibly can, at least, to as many servers to that the newsgroup is applicable. USENET does not need search engine indexing, even though Google has a comprehensive record of historical USENET articles.

Occasionally, Websites do not get indexed in any way, and that is where the DarkNet begins.

Not All Sinister

When Sites do not get indexed, it is generally because the webmaster was incompetent in some respect, since they did not put any effort into SEO or since there was no requirement to have the webpage indexed whatsoever. By way of instance, some research projects have sites dedicated to those who are only bibliographies or other stuff that nobody but participants will be interested in, so there is no use in getting those websites indexed whatsoever. The websites wind up floating around in the online ether, being of interest to anybody and are not actually picked up from the search engine crawlers. These websites become a part of this DarkNet.

You will also find countless websites that are started and left by webmasters and designers, usually amateurs. These websites wind up becoming a part of their DarkNet, especially when they are on hosting where they are never eliminated and where they simply sit indefinitely. Occasionally people encounter them and wind up finding resources that are interesting, sometimes not.

Some DarkNet websites are used for prohibited purposes. Still, there's not much likelihood that you are likely to stumble upon them. The search engines just don't possess them in their indicators; therefore, without typing the URL into your browser bar, you are not likely to locate them.

USENET is not a part of this DarkNet. USENET is transparent and can be made about sharing information, not concealing it. It is also something to which you get a subscription, so finding it's obviously not really that hard. The

USENET, nevertheless, has a massive backlog of archived posts and other information, which makes it as intriguing as any hidden portion of the web.

Safeguard Your Computer From Getting Hacked!

The Notion of people being worried that NSA is monitoring and listing their actions is a hysterically funny idea to me. Anything you think about Edward Snowden, understand he is a day late and a buck short. The majority of the exact same people who worry about the NSA, possess a"Tracebook", Twitter, Instagram or even a half a dozen additional societal networking accounts which need to be significantly decreasing the NSA budget. Actually, let us simply disband that the NSA and employ Google! It appears that the majority of us have zero matter publicly submitting our most intimate information about Facebook, including everything short of our Social Security numbers. Posting our existing place and"checking in" so the whole world knows not just where we are, however, what we're doing appears to be a totally crucial public support and should also have images of the meal I'm going to consume. Just how a lot of the very same people understand that each picture posted comprises Meta Data that also memorializes the GPS coordinates along with the camera kind used to select the picture? I know you need to talk about the image of their household, but you might not need ISIS to know precisely where they reside?

Everybody is willing to openly disclose this private information, it explains why so many stay ignorant of this data mining that goes on which you don't knowingly agree to. I suppose all of us know that Google is in the company of selling electronic consumer profiles for advertisers? Every kind an email to your friend about arranging a visit to Italy just to locate your inbox currently populated with traveling bureau"hot deals"? If your email doesn't fill up with travel deals to Italy, you can wager your online browser will now exhibit travel service ads, "learn to speak Italian." Best Italian Restaurants on each page you see fin! Ask me what we consider using Google Docs! We recommend that you contemplate DoNotTrackme extensions for your Chrome and Firefox browsers. Also, we advise that you set up"self-destructing biscuits" and observe how many cookies are exchanged together with your daily browser use. Bear in mind, we actually do not want your password and username we want your biscuits all of which are sent in clear text within which Starbucks wireless you've been using! All accessible using FireSheep!

Now, if This really is a vulnerability that impacts individuals, what exposure affects enterprise-level surroundings? Forget about the infamously leaking Windows Operating system along with your porous notebook, in the aftermath of this 55 Million credit card numbers stolen from Home Depot along with the 45 million stolen from Target, and we all have to be worried about the credit card machines in the checkout counter. Really the TJ Maxx heist has been in many ways much bigger! You may be contemplating how did the hackers undergo the Firewall? As we've pointed out previously, most pc network security exploitations aren't implemented through the firewall, as they are enforced by"social technology" with the help of a dumb employee or paid hitman. It's suspect at least one of those above-mentioned break-ins was aided with a third party trusted partners such as the heating and air-conditioning service company. Nothing like a hungry janitorial night service team to make a few added bucks plugging a USB device into any desktop, releasing a brand new and enhanced malware edition of BlackPOS! The majority of these stolen credit card numbers could be bought here or around the Darknet using a Tor browser to achieve silk street type sites.

It sounds You can not turn on a digital device now with no alerting you that a program upgrade is available for download.

In the TV set, to the cellular phone, tablet computers and even your vehicle, are subject to software upgrades. Can you question what's being downloaded to your device when you perform a software upgrade? You simply assume you're linking with Apple, Amazon or Samsung? Imagine if some wicked doer was actually only spoofing a software upgrade. You willingly downloaded a superb basket of spy goodies that turn on your mobile camera, then activate your mic and email snapshots back into the mother ship. NSA, are you kidding? You'd never understand if it was your partner or employer, could you? Nonetheless, millions of people do so without care, day after day and think nothing more about it. If you would like to be tracked anywhere you go, danger having your most romantic messages printed (simply ask Jenifer Lawrence and another star Naked hack sufferers) simply carry your Smartphone with you always!

Cyber-crime, Alongside the Ebola virus and violent terrorism, is the single most effectively damaging phenomenon to sabotage the American method of life because of the Cuban missile crisis. Nevertheless, the ordinary small business owner winces at the price of engaging a pc network security audit also believes that penetration testing is lovemaking foreplay. Whenever the IT team asks for a Firewall update or an increase in funds to pay a subscription to virus, spam and bot internet filtering that they can't justify the additional expense. Educating your employees on the safe use of the Internet over WiFi ought to be a part of their health preventive drug program. However, most companies will dismiss"social technology" vulnerabilities before significant data burglar publicly embarrasses them.

CHAPTER NINE
ALL ABOUT VPN

A virtual personal network (VPN) provides you online anonymity and privacy by developing a private system by a public online connection. VPNs conceal your internet protocol (IP) address so that your online activities are almost untraceable. Most significant, VPN services set encrypted and secure connections to provide better solitude than a bonded Wi-Fi hotspot.

Why would you need a VPN service?

Surfing the Net or transacting on an unsecured Wi-Fi system means you could Be exposing your personal info and surfing habits. That is the reason why a virtual private network, much better called a VPN, must be a must for anyone worried about their online privacy and security.

Think about all the times you have been on the move, reading emails while in line in the coffee shop, or assessing your bank account whilst waiting in the physician's office. Unless you're logged to a personal Wi-Fi system that demands a password, then any information sent during your internet session may be exposed to eavesdropping by strangers using the exact same network.

The anonymity and encryption of a VPN supply helps safeguard your internet Actions: sending emails, shopping online, or paying invoices. VPNs also keep your internet browsing anonymous.

The best way to VPN protects your IP address and solitude

VPNs basically create an info tunnel between your Regional network and also an exit Node in a different place, which may be thousands of kilometers apart, which makes it look like you're in a different location. This advantage allows online liberty or the capability to get your favorite programs and sites while on the move.

Following is a closer look at the way the virtual private network operates. VPNs use Encryption to scramble information when it is sent within a Wi-Fi system. Encryption makes the data unreadable. Data security is particularly important if using a people's Wi-Fi system since it prevents anyone else on your network from eavesdropping in your online activity.

There is another side to solitude. Without a VPN, your net service Supplier can understand your complete browsing history. Using a VPN, your search history is concealed. That is because your internet activity is going to be related to the VPN server's IP address, none. A VPN service provider can have servers throughout the world. That means your internet search action could seem to arise at any of these. Remember, search engines track your search history; however, they will connect that information with an IP address that is not yours. Again, your VPN will continue to keep your online activity confidential.

VPN solitude: What exactly does a VPN conceal?

A VPN can conceal a good deal of information that may put your privacy in danger. Here Are five of these.

1. Your surfing history

It is no secret where you go online. Your internet service provider, along with your internet browser, can monitor just about what that you do online. A whole lot of the sites you visit may also maintain a history. Web browsers may monitor your search history and connect that information for an IP address.

Listed below are just two examples of why You Might Want to maintain your surfing history private. Perhaps you've got a health condition and you are searching the internet for information regarding treatment choices. Guess what? Without a VPN, you have automatically shared that info. You might begin receiving targeted advertisements that could draw additional attention to your ailment.

Or perhaps you only wish to cost airline tickets for a trip next month. The Travel websites you see know you're searching for tickets plus they may exhibit fares, which are not the lowest price available.

These are only a few isolated cases. Remember that your internet Services Provider might have the ability to market your surfing history. Even so, personal browsers might not be entirely as private.

2. Your IP address and place

Anyone who catches your IP address may get what you've been hunting on The net and where you're situated when you hunted. Think about your IP address as the return address you would place in a letter. It leads back to your own device.

Since a VPN utilizes an IP address that is not your own, it allows you to Keep your internet privacy and hunt the internet anonymously. You are also protected against getting your search history accumulated, seen, or marketed. Bear in mind your search history may nevertheless be detected if you're using a public computer or one supplied by your employer, college, or other business.

3. Your place for streaming

You may cover streaming solutions that Allow You to see things such as Professional sports. When you travel away from the nation, the streaming service might not be accessible. There is a good explanation for this, such as contractual provisions and regulations in different countries. Nevertheless, a VPN will permit you to pick an IP address in your house country. That will offer you access to some occasions shown in your streaming support. You might also have the ability to steer clear of data or rate throttling.

4. Your apparatus

A VPN will help protect your devices, such as desktop, notebook, Tablet computer, and smart telephone, out of prying eyes. Your apparatus can be prime targets for cybercriminals if you get the world wide web, particularly if you're on a people's Wi-Fi system. Simply speaking, a VPN helps safeguard the information you send and get on your own apparatus so hackers will not have the ability to observe your every movement.

5. Your Internet activity -- to keep net liberty

Hopefully, you are not a candidate for government surveillance, but who knows. Keep in mind that a VPN protects from the online service provider seeing your surfing history. So you are protected in case a government service asks your online service provider to provide records of your online activity. Assuming your VPN supplier does not log your surfing history (some VPN suppliers do), your own VPN will help safeguard your net liberty.

How does a VPN help safeguard against identity theft?

Identity theft occurs when thieves steal your personal data and use It to commit crimes in your name -- such as taking over or opening new accounts, submitting tax returns on your title, or leasing or purchasing a property. A VPN will help safeguard against identity theft by helping to ensure your information. It generates an encrypted tunnel for the information you send and get that is out of range of cyberthieves.

In case your smartphone Wi-Fi is enabled in Any Way times, your apparatus could be Vulnerable without you knowing it. Regular tasks like online shopping, banking and surfing can expose your info, which makes you vulnerable to cybercrime.

A VPN can shield the information that you access or share together with your apparatus. That is particularly important if using a people's Wi-Fi system, in which a cyber thief about precisely the exact same network could catch your login credentials along with the credit card number you type in if you shop online.

You can not stop identity theft. Nobody can. Some safety aspects -- such as a Data breach with an organization in which you've got accounts -- are outside of your hands. However, a VPN will help protect the information that you send from and get on your own apparatus.

What should you look for at VPN services?

The VPN marketplace is packed with choices, so it is essential to Think about your needs when you are searching for a VPN.

Think of what's valuable to you. Would You like to be able to browse the Internet Anonymously by concealing your IP address? Are you fearful your advice could be stolen public Wi-Fi? Are you a frequent traveler that would like to have the ability to watch your favorite shows as you're on the move.

A Fantastic VPN can help you check all 3 boxes, but here are a few other points to think about.

The best way to Select a VPN

A wise way to remain protected when utilizing public Wi-Fi would be to use a VPN solution. However, what's the best way to decide on a digital private network? Below are a few questions to ask when you are choosing a VPN supplier.

Can they honor your own privacy? The purpose of using a VPN is to protect your privacy. Therefore your VPN supplier must respect your privacy, also. They ought to have a no-log policy, meaning that they never monitor or log on your online actions.

Can they operate the latest protocol? OpenVPN provides stronger security than other protocols, for example, PPTP. OpenVPN is an open-source program that supports all the significant operating systems.

Can they set information limitations? Depending upon your internet use, bandwidth might be a big deciding factor for you. Make sure their services fit your requirements by simply checking to see whether you will receive complete, unmetered bandwidth without data limitations.

Where are the servers located? Settle on which server places are essential for you too. If you would like to look as though you're accessing the internet from a specific locale, ensure that there's a host in that nation.

Are you going to be able to install VPN access on multiple devices? If you're like the average user, you generally use between five and three apparatus. Ideally, you would have the ability to use the VPN on all of them in precisely the exact same moment.

Just how much does it cost? If cost is important to you, then you might feel that a free VPN is the smartest choice. Bear in mind, however, that some VPN services might not charge you money. Still, you may "cover" in different manners, like being served regular ads or using your personal information collected and marketed to third parties. Should you compare paid free options, You Might Discover That complimentary VPNs:

do not provide the maximum current or protected

protocols

do not provide the Maximum bandwidth and connection rates to free customers

do possess a Greater disconnection speed

do not have as many servers at as many nations internationally

do not provide support

There are many factors to consider when you're selecting a VPN, so do your own homework to ensure that you're getting the ideal match for your requirements. Irrespective of which supplier you choose, rest assured that a great VPN provides more protection, privacy, and anonymity on the web than the usual public Wi-Fi hotspot can.

VPN glossary

Learning VPNs may look like it needs a technical language. Following is a glossary with definitions of a few of the most common terms you will see.

AES encryption

Encryption is Vital to keep your information unreadable by hackers, Private businesses, and government agencies. Encryption jumbles your information so that others can not make sense of it without the particular decryption key. AES, which stands for Advanced Encryption Standard, has been an encryption system developed by Belgium cryptographers Joan Daemen and Vincent Rijmen. In 2002, AES became the U.S. national standard for encryption. It has since been the typical type of encryption for the remainder of the planet, too.

Browser background

An inventory of your online activity using a Specific browser, Including keywords you hunted and sites you obtained.

Geo-restrictions

Among the chief reasons, users rely on VPNs? They Wish to Avoid geo-restrictions. These constraints are usually set up by entertainment companies that just need to distribute articles to specific areas. For example, Netflix may offer content from the United States it does not show in the united kingdom. It may provide programming in the UK which Netflix users from the USA can not get. By making use of a VPN using an IP address established in the united kingdom, U.S. audiences can attempt to get Netflix programming which is not available in their home nation. The VPN support -- as well as the VPN link -- hides the place where the reliable online connection is created. Assess your streaming support arrangement because of its Conditions of Service, and be aware that some nations might have penalties for using VPN to bypass its own rules.

Google search history

A record of your online searches using the Google search engine optimization.

IP address

IP stands for Internet Protocol, along with an IP address is a series of amounts And intervals that defines a computer that is using the Internet Protocol to send and receive information within a network.

IPsec

IPsec is a series of protocols, or principles, which virtual private networks utilize To secure a personal link between two things, usually a device like a smartphone or notebook and the world wide web. With no protocols, VPNs wouldn't have the ability to encrypt information and make sure the information privacy of consumers. The title IPsec stands for Internet Protocol Security.

ISP

Short for Internet Service Provider, this is a service that you pay for to Connect to the web. ISPs can document your surfing history and might have the ability to market it to third parties, such as advertising or other functions.

Kill change

Users sign up using a VPN provider for internet privacy and information protection. However, What happens when a VPN provider's network link fails? Your computer or Mobile device will return to the public IP address supplied by your ISP. This means your online activity can now be monitored. A kill button, however, Prevents this from occurring. If your VPN supplier's connection fails, then the Kill-switch attribute severs your link to the web completely. This Manner, your online activities will not be tracked by other people. Not all VPN suppliers Provide this attribute, so search for this when searching around.

L2TP

The acronym L2TP stands for the Layer 2 Tunneling Protocol. It is a series of Rules that allow online service providers to allow for VPNs. L2TP by itself, though, doesn't encrypt data, so it does not offer complete privacy for users. That's why L2TP is usually used with IPsec to help protect the online privacy of users.

Public Wi-Fi

A wireless community in a public location that allows you to connect a pc Or other apparatus to the internet. Public Wi-Fi is frequently unprotected and potentially accessible to hackers.

Search engines

A service that allows you to look for information using keywords on the internet. Many popular search engines record your search history and can earn money off that information.

Service supplier

A Business that Offers a virtual private network -- basically routing your Link through a distant server and encrypting the information.

Simultaneous connections

You probably have plenty of devices connected to the net at any one time, everything out of the smartphone to your notebook to the desktop computer in your house office. Many VPN providers now offer protection for all your simultaneous internet connections with a single account. That is important: You might think of log to a VPN before hunting the net in your notebook. But if your smartphone is not protected by a secure

VPN, your surfing activity on such apparatus will not have security.

Virtual private community

A VPN gives you online anonymity and privacy by creating a private network From a public internet connection. It pushes your internet protocol address to maintain your internet actions private. It provides encrypted and secure links to provide increased privacy and security for the data you send and receive.

VPN connection

A virtual private network link Permits You to access the internet Through a remote server, concealing your real location and browser history, and encrypting your data.

VPN privacy

This refers to the solitude that having a VPN provides. For instance, a VPN Encrypts your information, disguises your own location, and hides your browsing history and the data you transmit through the internet.

VPN customers

A VPN client makes it easier for users to link to a virtual private network. That's as it's the actual software that is installed on your pc, tablet or phone. The most common operating systems, such as Android, Windows, and iOS, come with VPN client applications pre-installed. But many users decide to work with third-party VPN clients offering different characteristics and user interfaces.

VPN protocols

VPN protocols are similar to a pair of instructions. VPN providers utilize these Protocols to make sure that users can connect securely to a virtual private network. There are several VPN protocols available, all with their particular strengths and weaknesses. OpenVPN is just one of the more popular protocols. Users enjoy OpenVPN because it's secure and works with most operating systems. The biggest downside of OpenVPN? It can offer slower link rates than other protocols.

VPN supplier

Synonymous with VPN Support, this really is a service you sign up for that allows You to connect to a virtual private network by providing a temporary IP address that hides your actual address.

VPN server

VPN services Permit You to connect to the internet through

remote servers That they either have or have access to. This disguises your location.

VPN support

An agency you sign up for this allows you to link to a virtual personal Network by giving a temporary IP address that hides your dedicated address.

VPN tunnel

You may sometimes hear your virtual personal network Known as a VPN tunnel. This is only another name for the encrypted connection between your device -- a notebook, phone, tablet or desktop computer -- and the internet. You can make a VPN tunnel in your home or on public Wi-Fi. As soon as you are using a VPN tunnel to connect to the world wide web, your ISP, private companies, or the government can't observe the sites you're browsing or the links you're clicking. A VPN tunnel also hides your IP address. Instead of showing your real place, the websites you browse is only going to register the position of this VPN supplier with which you are working.

VPN web browser

An Internet browser that includes a built-in VPN service, allowing you to conceal Your browsing activity online.

Search history

A record of everything you searched for on the world wide web. Your internet service provider and your internet browser probably have a complete history of your search action.

Wi-Fi

A wireless system using a radio frequency to connect your own pc and Other devices on the internet and each other.

CHAPTER TEN
HOW TO USE TOR

As of late, BoingBoing ran an article about how a few custodians in Massachusetts were introducing Tor programming in the entirety of their open PCs to anonymize the perusing propensities for their supporters. The curators are doing this as a remain against detached government observation just as organizations that track clients on the web and construct dossiers to serve profoundly focused on promoting.

It's a fascinating venture, and a strong represent client protection. However, fortunately, if you need to peruse secretly, you don't need to go to the library to utilize Tor. Associating with the Tor arrange from your own PC is fast and easy gratitude to the Tor undertaking's dead straightforward Tor Browser.

What is Tor?

Tor is a PC arrange run by volunteers around the world. Each volunteer runs what is known as a hand-off, which is only a PC that runs programming enabling clients to associate with the Internet through the Tor arrange.

Before hitting the open Internet, the Tor Browser will interface with a few distinct transfers, cleaning its tracks at all times, making it hard to make sense of where, and who, you truly are.

While Tor is increasing notoriety for being a device for purchasing illegal products on the web, the work has various authentic employments. Activists covering their area from severe systems and writers speaking with unknown sources are two straightforward models.

On the off chance that similar to the bookkeepers in Massachusetts, you don't have an outlandish purpose behind utilizing Tor, it's as yet a decent device to keep your perusing private from your ISP, promoters, or inactive government information assortment. In any case, if the NSA or other three-letter office chose to effectively focus on your perusing propensities that is an entire distinctive ballgame.

Beginning

The most straightforward approach to utilize Tor is to download the Tor Browser. This is an altered variant of Firefox alongside a lot of other programmings that associates you to the Tor organize.

When you've downloaded the installer, you have two choices: You can simply introduce the product or you can check the establishment record's GPG signature first. A few people like to check the establishment document to ensure they've downloaded the best possible rendition of the program and not something that has been messed with.

However, checking the GPG mark is anything but an effortless procedure and requires an extra programming download. By and by, if that is something you'd prefer to do, the Tor Project has a how-to clarifying what's needed.

If you need to keep your web perusing private, you can utilize the Incognito mode in Chrome, Private Browsing in Firefox, InPrivate mode in Microsoft Edge, etc. While this will forestall others who use your PC from seeing your perusing history, it doesn't keep your ISP from observing the destinations you are visiting. You may well need to – for any number of reasons – peruse the web totally namelessly, and this is absolutely what Tor Browser offers.

Representing The Onion Router, Tor offers different degrees of assurance to guarantee that your online exercises, area and personality are kept totally private. Here are the means you have to follow to introduce and utilize Tor Browser.

1. Introduce and design Tor Browser

Start by downloading and introducing Tor Browser. Snap Finish once the establishment is finished, and Tor will dispatch just because. You'll be welcomed by a settings discourse that is utilized to control how you associate with the Tor arrange.

Much of the time you ought to have the option to simply tap the Connect button, yet on the off chance that you associate with the web through an intermediary you should tap the Configure catch to enter your settings.

2. Get online with Tor

There will be a slight postponement while Tor sets up an association with the system through transfers – the program cautions that the underlying association could take up to a few minutes – however once this association has been made, the Tor program will dispatch prepared for use.

Tor depends on a similar code as Firefox, so on the off chance that you have utilized Mozilla's internet browser everything ought to appear to be genuinely natural. Regardless of whether you haven't utilized Firefox previously, it ought not to take you well before you begin to feel comfortable – it's not all that not the same as any semblance of Edge, Chrome and Safari.

3. Pick your security level

Before you begin, it's important that utilizing Tor Browser is an exercise in careful control between protection/security and web convenience. As a matter of course, security is set to Standard – even though this is still undeniably more secure than some other internet browser.

If you might want to expand this, click the onion symbol to one side of the location bar and choose Security Settings. Utilize the Security Level slider to pick your favored degree of assurance, remembering the alerts that show up about the highlights that may quit taking a shot at the locales you visit.

4. Reexamine your perusing propensities

To take full advantage of Tor, you have to change a couple of your perusing propensities – the first of these is the internet searcher you use.

As opposed to deciding on any semblance of Google and Bing, the proposal is that you first go to Disconnect.me. This is a website that avoids web crawlers from following you on the web, and you can utilize it related to Bing, Yahoo or DuckDuckGo.

While we're regarding the matter of evolving propensities, you additionally need to abstain from introducing program augmentations, as these can release private data.

5. Comprehend Tor circuits

As you peruse the web, the Tor program keeps you secure by maintaining a strategic distance from legitimately interfacing with sites. First, your association is ricocheted around between various hubs on the Tor arrange, with each hop highlighting anonymizing.

This makes everything as well as inconceivable for a site to follow who and where you are, it is likewise liable for the marginally moderate presentation you will see while perusing with Tor.

On the off chance that you feel execution is uncommonly low or a page is never again reacting, you can begin another Tor circuit by tapping the cheeseburger symbol and choosing the 'New Tor Circuit for this Site' alternative, which will constrain Tor to locate another course to the site.

6. Make another character

The new circuit choice just applies to the present dynamic tab, and it might be that you need an increasingly extraordinary protection wellbeing net. Snap the cheeseburger symbol and select 'New Identity', remembering that this will close and restart Tor so as to get another IP address.

At the point when you interface with a site utilizing Tor, you may see that a popup seems cautioning you that a specific site is attempting to accomplish something that might be utilized to follow you. Exactly how regularly these messages show up will depend on the locales you visit, yet in addition the protection settings you have set up.

7. Use HTTPS

A significant piece of remaining sheltered and mysterious online is guaranteeing that you utilize the HTTPS instead of HTTP forms of sites. So you don't need to make sure to do this for each site you visit, Tor Browser accompanies the HTTPS Everywhere expansion introduced as a matter of course. This will attempt to divert you to the protected variant of any site in the event that it is accessible, yet you should watch out for the location bar as an additional defend.

On the off chance that you are associated with a protected site, you will see a green lock symbol. If this is absent, click the 'I' symbol for more data.

8. Access .onion destinations

The most secure approach to interface with the web through Tor, nonetheless, is to visit .onion locales. These are otherwise called concealed Tor administrations, and they are out of reach to web crawlers; to discover them, you need to visit them legitimately.

To assist you with finding such locales, there are various .onion catalogs out there. These destinations must be gotten to utilizing Tor. Yet, you do need to fare thee well – it's elementary to go over locales with illegal substances, selling illicit items or advancing criminal operations.

9. Attempt Tor over VPN

On the off chance that you need to take your protection to the following level, you can interface with a VPN before beginning the Tor program. The VPN won't have the option to perceive what you're doing in the Tor program, and you'll get the additional advantage that no Tor hub will have the option to see your IP address. It will likewise keep your system administrators from realizing that you are utilizing Tor, which is useful if the Tor Network happens to be blocked where you are.

DIFFERENCES BETWEEN TOR i2p and Freenet

The 3 significant obscurity organizes on the Internet are Tor/Onionland, I2P and Freenet. On the off chance that you feel befuddled on which one is the "best" one to utilize the appropriate response is essential. Utilize each of the three!

Every secrecy organize is intended for an alternate explicit reason. One system alone can't do what the three can do together. Tor and I2P can't endure data like Freenet can; Tor and Freenet can't offer the nonexclusive vehicles that I2P gives and Freenet doesn't deal with information gushing just as Tor and I2P. There is likewise no preferable intermediary framework over the Tor organization.

Tor/Onionland

Tor is a mysterious Internet intermediary. You intermediary through various Tor transfers and in the long run go through a Tor leave hand-off that enables traffic to exit out of Tor and into the Internet. Tor has the most consideration and the most help. The client base on the Tor arrange is by and large 100,000 to 200,000 clients in size which is the biggest of the three. Tor likewise gives a mysterious intranet frequently alluded to as Onionland.

Onionland utilizes a similar strategy to associate with a machine distinguished by a cryptographic open key. Along these lines you can only with significant effort decide the machine's IP address.

Positive Parts of Tor/Onionland:

Written In C, that implies that it is quick and by and large low memory use.

Easy and straightforward UI. Vidalia, the Tor control programming, is a straight point and snap.

Generally complex and robust framework for proxying right now concocted.

Negative Parts of Tor/Onionland:

Written in C. The source code tree of any undertaking written in C is always enormous and challenging to make sense of what is happening. C is a low level incorporated framework language. More exertion is expected to anticipate memory releases, support floods and similarity with various designs and working frameworks. There is nothing of the sort as a little C program, with C there is always many more lines.

Restricted Functionality. In any event, including the concealed administration's usefulness, Tor still doesn't do particularly alongside go about as a mysterious intermediary.

The system is packed. The Core framework of Tor is 2,500 to 3,000 machines directing traffic and has 100,000 to 200,000 clients consistently. Onionland has less secrecy versus I2P. With Tor you are focusing on all things considered 3,000 machines. I2P as of March 2012 has expected multiple times the number of machines directing data. Contingent upon the day, I2P has an expected 9,000 to 14,000 dynamic machines. Even though 14,000 is the total of I2P, regardless, you have to manage multiple occasions more devices versus Onionland when doing assaults.

Associations with Tor aren't dynamic like I2P burrows are, Tor circuits continue until shutting. This can lessen obscurity.

No help for UDP

The best use for Tor is mysteriously proxying to the standard Internet.

FreeNet

Freenet is mysterious information distributing Network and is altogether different from Tor and I2P. Freenet is a lot higher inertness and concentrates more on a companion to companion collaborations with regular military evaluation security. To play off of an old Internet image...

Freenet is a significant truck you dump stuff on, while I2P is a progression of Tubes.

Freenet utilizes UDP and is the "most established" of the 3 Networks. It is difficult to measure the size of Freenet on account of its capacity to interface only to companions and not outsiders. It's assessed to have around 20,000 dynamic machines yet may have more.

Positive Parts of FreeNet:

Better Friend Than Friend Sharing versus I2P.

The "most secure" of all the 3 systems for distributing content secretly.

Simple Setup.

Negative Parts of Freenet:

Slow, and VERY asset escalated. Written In Java.

Requires the client penance transmission capacity as well as room on your hard drive.

Freenet is a device for bypassing extremist control where individuals would be executed for distributing certain substances. Hence, it's NOT for easygoing perusing.

The best use is distributing content secretly.

I2P (Invisible Internet Project)

I2P is a Distributed Peer to Peer Anonymous Network Layer. It enables you to send information between PCs running I2P secretly with a multilayer start to finish encryption. I2P got from IIP (Invisible IRC Project) which was one of FreeNet's sister ventures. I2P centers around only inward correspondence and not proxying to the customary Internet. I2P utilizes garlic directing, which includes amassing parcels together into more excellent bundles. The mix of garlic steering, multilayer encryption and irregular cushioning on bundles makes an examination of the substance and location of the beginning of I2P traffic exceptionally unreasonable if not about inconceivable. I2P right now has 9,000 to 14,000 dynamic machines relying upon the hour of the day. The greater part of the hubs is either European or Russian.

Positive Parts of I2P:

Can do everything the ordinary Internet can do. Downpours, HTTP, or some other TCP or UDP based convention. Client Defined Transport Layer conventions could also be utilized if you know some Java.

All around Documented API for building applications that utilization I2P

Assorted, Interesting and proficient network.

Negative Parts of I2P:

New clients need to hold back to get quicker speeds and it is still not as quick as Tor can be

Asset Intensive, not as awful as FreeNet yet at the same time not on a par with Tor. Written in Java.

Exploratory programming, as yet being effectively created and is viewed as beta programming.

Needs academic analysis on the level that tor has gotten.

The client gathering isn't yet as noob agreeable like Tor.

The best use for I2P is for distributed document sharing and trade for the standard Internet if it gets awful enough to warrant such activity

The Phantom Protocol

From what I can assemble, the apparition convention is only that, a ghost. After extensive periods almost no advancement was made on its improvement. It appears vaporware to me and I have next to no to say about it.

End

There is nobody Anonymity Network that "does everything." To have viable obscurity you should adapt something other than one device. Regardless of whether you figure out how to utilize the 3 systems appropriately, there is still significantly more to learn. Each system has its various utilizations. There are many more instruments that can be used with these systems to give substantially greater usefulness that go past this concise outline. Such including progressed ssh burrowing and design, individual VPNs and many order line devices that when utilized together, can accomplish beyond what most normal clients can with GUI based instruments. Secrecy arranges right presently are the likened to the Internet in the mid-1990s, a "realm of programmers" needing to make a superior tomorrow.

Do Not Go Yet; One Last Thing To Do!

If you enjoyed this book or found it useful, I'd be very grateful if you'd post a short review on Amazon.

Your support really does make a difference, and I read all the reviews personally so I can get your feedback and make this book even better.

Thanks again for your support!

Sam

ABOUT THE AUTHOR

Samuel K. is an ethical hacker who has been active on the net for more than 20 years. He has been a cybersecurity consultant for many government agencies and therefore he prefers to remain anonymous because of the information in this book. We only know he's married and has a dog, Maggie.

His favorite phrase is:
"If you can do it today, don't wait for tomorrow."